Victorious Bible Curriculum

THE BEGINNING (PART 1 OF 9)

God created a home for mankind, and placed us in it to tend and guard it as His image. When we rebelled, God promised a seed of the woman to one day restore creation — and preserved that seed when our violence filled the world.

THE PATRIARCHS (PART 2 OF 9)

God chose Abraham to be the custodian of the line through which the promised redeemer would come. Abraham's grandson Jacob became the father of the twelve tribes of Israel, a nation that would bless the whole earth.

THE EXODUS (PART 3 OF 9)

For 400 years, God grew Jacob's tiny family into a nation. Through Moses, He released them from slavery to give them a new home. Despite the faithless first generation's rebellion, their children would inherit the promised land.

CONQUEST AND JUDGMENT (PART 4 OF 9)

Under Joshua, the children of the exodus conquered the promised land. After they settled in, they fell into idolatry and suffered under foreign domination. Time after time, they needed God's deliverance through a head-crushing judge.

THE KINGDOM OF ISRAEL (PART 5 OF 9)

God used Israel's first kings, the vacillating Saul and the head-crusher David, to give Israel peace. Solomon built a prosperous kingdom, which then split and fell into idolatry. After 70 years' exile in Babylon, God restored them to the land.

THE COMING OF THE MESSIAH (PART 6 OF 9)

The long wait for the serpent-crushing redeemer came to an end with the birth of Jesus of Nazareth. Raised in Galilee and baptized in the Jordan, He began to proclaim the kingdom of God and demonstrate God's love and power.

THE MINISTRY OF JESUS (PART 7 OF 9)

The blind could see, the sick were healed, the dead raised. The kingdom of God was truly at hand. But the leaders of Israel rejected the One God had sent to save them from their sins and deliver them into God's kingdom.

JESUS' FINAL DAYS (PART 8 OF 9)

On Thursday, before His arrest, Jesus ate one final meal with His disciples. Then He was arrested, beaten, falsely accused, tried, convicted and crucified. But death could not hold Him and the grave could not contain Him.

THE BEGINNING OF THE CHURCH (PART 9 OF 9)

After His resurrection, Jesus' followers received the power of the Holy Spirit to disciple the nations of the world, baptizing them and teaching them all that Jesus had said. Christ's body grew and began to crush the enemy's head under her feet.

Copyright © 2017 by Joe Anderson and Tim Nichols

All rights reserved
Printed in the United States of America
First Edition

No part of this book may be reproduced in any form or by any electronic or mechanical means, including information storage and retrieval systems, except for brief quotations in printed reviews, without the prior permission of the author.

Unless otherwise indicated, all Scripture quotations are taken from the New King James Version®. Copyright © 1982 by Thomas Nelson, Inc. Used by permission. All rights reserved.

Scripture quotations marked (NIV) are taken from the Holy Bible, New International Version®, NIV®. Copyright © 1973, 1978, 1984, 2011 by Biblica, Inc.™ Used by permission of Zondervan. All rights reserved worldwide. www.zondervan.com The "NIV" and "New International Version" are trademarks registered in the United States Patent and Trademark Office by Biblica, Inc.™

Author's translation or paraphrase indicated by an asterisk after the reference.

Illustrations by Gustave Doré
Colorized and modified by William Britton

Praise for Headwaters Bible Curriculum

These lessons are not just a way to teach the Bible to middle school kids. As I read the lessons, I found both my head and my heart irresistibly engaged. Joe and Tim have opened the grace and truth of God's Word in a way that seriously lifts us towards Christ while nudging us outward towards the world. I recommend these studies for both devotional and motivational reading!

Dave Cheadle, President of the Rocky Mountain Classis, Reformed Church of America

While I have spent quite a bit of time studying the Bible myself, I find your ideas and themes to be real food for thought and they help tie together much of the story God is telling throughout... I've already talked with people about your curriculum and have recommended they look into it for their own families. I can't loan out my copy for their perusal, because I'm using it everyday!

Linda Kidder, Home Educator, Colorado

I LOVE THIS BOOK!!!! We're just finishing up the Garden narrative. We've had such fruitful discussions—I have been pleased with it in every way. In fact, I'm hoping our church will start using it. I haven't had any problems or difficulties using the curriculum, I ONLY have good things to say about it. In fact, I'm in danger of writing in all caps I'm so enthusiastic about it.

Leah Robinson, Home Educator, Texas

I am really enjoying having this resource to work from and steer our lessons!

Christy Johnson, Bible Teacher, Bingham Academy, Ethiopia

Our family actually loves the curriculum. My children are in 5th and 8th grade and the content has suited both of their levels perfectly. To this point we hadn't found a curriculum that taught the Bible at such a detailed level that has also kept the kids engaged. We've had to slow down on the materials because otherwise they would be through them well before the school year is up. We are planning on buying the rest of the series.

Chris Turner, Home Educator, Colorado

How to Use This Book

This series of little manuals walks you through the biblical Story from end to end. Just read. Here are a few things you might want to keep in mind as you read through the Story.

- Try to love the characters. God does....
- The story is written in such a way as to make sin look stupid, but remember that the characters are all real people. No matter how stupid the choice, a real person actually looked at the options and then picked that particular one for reasons that seemed pretty good at the time. Nobody gets up in the morning and says, "I'm going to make stupid life choices that people will be mocking for centuries." Try to see it from their point of view. Ask yourself, "Why did this look like a good idea at the time?" That's how you learn to recognize temptations. It's easy to see sinful and stupid choices for what they are in hindsight, but in the moment it's often very hard. So learn to think through what these choices looked like from the inside, in the heat of the moment — you'll be amazed what you learn about yourself.
- Pay attention to the patterns. We'll point out a bunch of them as we go through the Story, but try to spot them yourself, too. If you can learn to read the Word and see the patterns in the Story, you will become able to read the world around you and see the patterns in the story God is telling right now.
- In the Old Testament curriculum, every lesson came with a Psalm. Not all of the New Testament lessons do, but you should know enough about how to connect the Psalms to the Story that you can discover your own connections. If there is no Psalm provided, feel free to take some time to read through a few Psalms and try to find one that fits. You'll be surprised what you can learn.
- As with any book that talks about Scripture, don't necessarily take our word for anything. Imagine you're sitting in a living room or around a campfire with us, and we're just talking about the Story. You're free to disagree, correct, challenge our understanding. The Word is the authority, not us — so grab your Bible and look things up yourself.

You'll find a section labeled "Activities" following the lesson. The point of this section is to immerse you as deeply in the Story as possible, through prayer, meditation on the Story, and other exercises. The "Evaluation" questions at the end of each lesson will help you to check your understanding of the material.

For Small Group Leaders
Have everyone in the group read the lesson ahead of time. Depending on how involved your group is, you can have them engage some or all of the activities, or you can save those for group time when you're together. The evaluation questions might serve as discussion starters if the conversation lags.

Table of Contents

Unit 1 The Incarnation of Christ 7
    Lesson 1.1 The Times of the Gentiles (Intertestamental Period) 9
    Lesson 1.2 The New Creation 17
    Lesson 1.3 The Seed-Line: The New Adam and Son of David 23
    Lesson 1.4 Miraculous Births: John and Jesus 29
    Lesson 1.5 Jesus' Flight to Egypt: Jesus is the New Israel 37
    Lesson 1.6 The Foreshadowing of Jesus' Temple Ministry 45

Unit 2 Jesus' Ministry Begins 51
    Lesson 2.1 The Ministry of John the Baptist 53
    Lesson 2.2 Jesus' Baptism 59
    Lesson 2.3 Jesus' Fasting and Temptation 67
    Lesson 2.4 John Passed the Baton to Jesus 75
    Lesson 2.5 Water into Wine 81
    Lesson 2.6 From Darkness to Light: Jesus and Nicodemus 87
    Lesson 2.7 The Woman at the Well 95

UNIT 1: THE INCARNATION OF CHRIST

As God had promised, Israel returned to the land after 70 years of captivity, but things were not the same as before. Israel was under the rule of a series of Gentile empires and had a new calling—instead of manifesting God's holiness through their distinctions as a separate nation, they were to shine their light from within these worldly empires. Many Jews couldn't figure out how to be in the world but not of it and either imitated the world they lived in or separated themselves from it completely.

Into this world, Jesus the Messiah was born in a stable in Bethlehem. He was the Savior Israel had been long awaiting… but He didn't come as a conquering king as they had been expecting. He came as a baby—the One who had been with God in the beginning speaking the world into existence. He was the promised Son, the culmination of the seed-line, the new Adam, the Son of Abraham and the promised Son of David. Jesus was the new Samuel, the miraculously conceived supplanter of priests. And His cousin, John the Baptist was the new Samson, the miraculously conceived forerunner called to prepare the way for the Messiah.

The word of the coming of the King could not be concealed. Being guided by a star, Magi from the east made their way to Israel to meet the Messiah. When they arrived in Jerusalem, they told Herod that the King had arrived and asked where He was. Herod hoped to learn more about the location of the Messiah from the Magi so he could have Him killed, but the Magi outwitted Herod and returned to the east by a different route. Jesus and His family had to flee their home to be saved from the murderous king, like Israel had under Pharaoh. Jesus is the new Israel.

As Jesus grew, He also began to fulfill His role as the new Samuel. Even as a 12-year-old, Jesus spent time in His true Father's house, questioning and answering the priests. Ultimately, He would question the priests so much that they would arrest Him and put Him to death. After His resurrection, He would ascend to His Father's right hand and supplant the wicked priests.

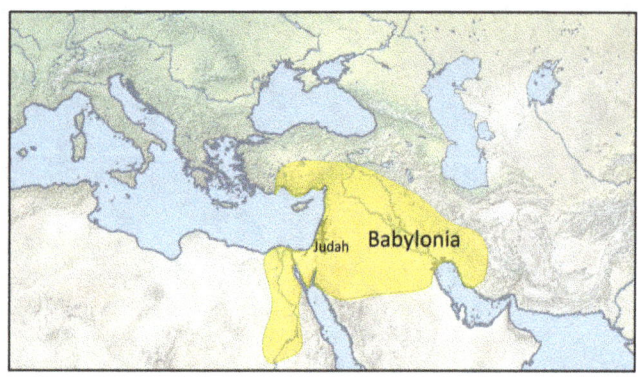

BABYLONIA (626-539 B.C.)

- Head of gold in Daniel's statue
- Destroyed Jerusalem and the temple and carried Judah into captivity in 586 B.C.

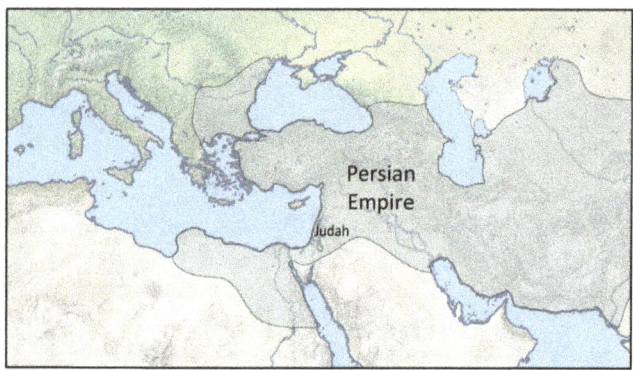

PERSIAN EMPIRE (539-332 BC)

- Chest and arms of silver in Daniel's statue
- Darius captured Babylon in 539 B.C.

GREEK EMPIRE (332-63 BC)

- Belly and thighs of bronze in Daniel's statue
- Alexander the Great defeated the Persians in 332 B.C.

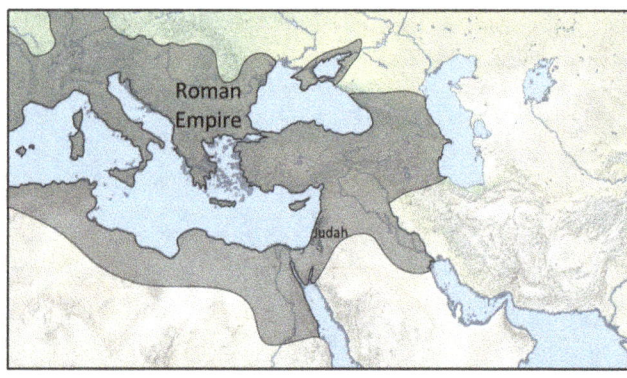

ROMAN EMPIRE (63 BC- 476 AD)

- Legs of iron and feet of iron and clay in Daniel's statue
- Roman General Pompey conquered Jerusalem in 63 B.C.

LESSON 1.1

The Times of the Gentiles (Intertestamental Period)

UNIT 1

NOTES TO THE TEACHER

Lesson Theme - God prepared the world for the coming of Christ.

This lesson covers the period of time between the Old Testament (the return of exile) to the New Testament (the birth of Christ). This period is often skipped, presumably because the Bible doesn't specifically address it. In reality, a good portion of Daniel's prophecies address this period. Furthermore, some very important changes happened between the testaments that prepared the world for the coming of the Messiah.

After Cyrus, king of Persia, defeated Babylon, he issued a decree that the people of Judah who had been carried captive to Babylon should return to the land and rebuild the temple (Ezra 1). This happened 70 years after the Babylonian captivity in fulfillment of God's promise that it was a 70 year exile (Jer 29:10). Under great opposition, the people of Judah rebuilt the temple and the walls of Jerusalem and returned to the worship of Yahweh (see OT Lesson 9.4).

Daniel remained in captivity, but wrote a number of prophecies pertaining to this period. The first prophecy came through Nebuchadnezzar. He had a dream (recorded in Dan 2) of a giant statue with a head of gold, chest and arms of silver, belly and thighs of bronze, legs of iron and feet of iron and clay. Nebuchadnezzar saw a rock strike the feet of the statue, and the entire statue turned to dust and blew away. Daniel explained that Babylon was the head of gold and a series of successive kingdoms were the other sections of the statute.

OVERVIEW

Israel returned to the land and rebuilt the temple and the walls of Jerusalem 70 years after their captivity—as God had promised. Upon their return, however, they found a sort of new world order. Israel had been an independent nation called to shine their light out to other nations. Now, they were under the control of Gentile kingdoms and were to shine their light from within. Instead of faithfully shining that light, however, the people fell into two different traps. Some clothed themselves with the culture and customs of their Gentile lords such that they were indistinguishable from those whom they were called to reach. Others separated themselves so that the Gentiles *could not* be invited into a relationship with God. During this time, God was preparing the world for Jesus who would show Israel a new way of shining the light, a way that was faithful to the Old Testament Law and faithful to shine the light to the nations.

SOURCE MATERIAL

- Daniel 2:31-45, 11:1-39
- Psalm 137
- *Rose Book of Bible Charts, Maps and Timelines*, pages 68-72
- *The Four* by Peter Leithart, Chapter 1 (for further study)

Unit 1: The Incarnation of Christ

OBJECTIVES

Feel...

- a sense that everything was changing in preparation for Jesus.
- sadness at so much pain and oppression in Israel.
- distress that Israel fell into the extremes of separateness and accommodation without learning how to shine their light.

Understand...

- the broad succession of events in the intertestamental period and their relationship to Daniel's statue.
- how Israel gained independence through the Maccabean revolt.
- that Israel was under the dominion of the increasingly tyrannical Hasmonean dynasty.
- who Herod the Great was and how he prepared the world for Jesus.
- that Israel went from shining their light out to the Gentiles to shining their light from within.
- that Israel fell into the two extremes of separation and isolation or accommodation to the Greek way of life.
- that all of this prepared the way for Jesus to demonstrate how to shine the light and prepared the world for the missionary work of the Church.

Apply this understanding by...

- looking at your life in terms of separation versus accommodation to the world and evaluating if you are more tempted to separate from the world or more tempted to act like the world.

Later, after Persia (the silver kingdom) had defeated the Babylonians (539 B.C), Daniel received a vision in which an angel explained in more detail how each of these kingdoms would come to be. This prophecy is recorded in Daniel 11.

Daniel records that three more Persian kings would come; then a mighty Greek king would defeat the Persians and expand the kingdom of Greece (Dan 11:1-3, 336-326 B.C.). This was a reference to Alexander the Great. That kingdom, however, would be split up after Alexander's death (Dan 11:4, 323 B.C.). Daniel records that two of these mini-kingdoms would exert particular influence: the king of the south—the Ptolemies in Egypt, and the king of the north—the Seleucids based in Syria. Israel was caught right in between these battling kingdoms and was initially ruled by the Ptolemies, but was later taken under the control of the Seleucids.

Through all of this kingdom upheaval, Israel was under great pressure to conform to the Greek way of life which became a source of tension among the Jews. Some fell into the trap of fully taking on the culture of their civil rulers. Others fell into the opposite trap and completely separated from the people God was calling them to reach. Eventually, Antiochus IV, the ruler of the Seleucids, forced all Jews to abandon their own culture and take on the Greek culture. Many did, but others found the strength to resist in the face of death. Antiochus even entered into the temple and offered a sacrifice to Zeus.

Daniel prophesied that at this point Israel would receive a "little help" (Dan 11:34). This help came in the form of a revolt against their oppressors and the Jews who had joined them. One of Antiochus' officials visited a small village called Modir and tried to force the Jews there to offer a sacrifice to Greek gods. A priest named Mattathias refused to join in and even killed a Jewish priest who had offered the sacrifice as well as the official overseeing the whole thing. Mattathias and his five sons fled to the mountains where Mattathias died.

His son, Judah, called Maccabeus (which means "hammer") took up his father's call to battle. Judah was a great military commander and successfully defeated the local Seleucid force (while Antiochus was off fighting Persia with the Seleucid army). The Maccabees also took some additional territory around the land that they had lost to their enemies. The Maccabean successors held onto the ground that Judah gained, but the nation was still split. Many Jews were fine with the Greek customs; thus, the Jewish factions within the land were in great tension. Furthermore, the Maccabees set themselves up as priests, and while they *were* Levites, they *were not* of the line of Zadok which God had said were to fulfill the high priestly role after the exile. The Maccabean revolt took place from 167-160 B.C.

The Maccabean line became the priest-kings of Israel and were referred to as the Hasmonean dynasty (140-63 B.C.). However, it didn't take long before the Hasmoneans turned into tyrants. One of the most oppressive Hasmoneans, Alexander, killed 6,000 Jews in battle, had 800 rebels crucified, and ordered that their children's throats be cut before the eyes of their mothers. Eventually, the Hasmonean dynasty came to an end in civil war.

When the Hasmonean dynasty fell apart, the Romans took control of Israel (63 B.C.). The land was split up among different local rulers. During the takeover, a new player, Antipater, seized some political authority and gained control of portions of Israel. His son, Herod, rode on his coattails and proved to be an adept politician under the new Roman kingdom (Daniel's iron kingdom). Herod the Great exalted himself as a god and is spoken of as the ultimate self-exalting king in Daniel 11:36-37. Herod was a new Saul; and Jesus, the new David, was born into a world where he was king.

In addition to all that political tension, Israel had developed a complex set of religious tensions within Judaism. Some Jews had attempted to separate themselves from the Gentile influence. One sect, the Essenes, had moved into the Dead Sea wilderness and created a "pure" Jewish community. The Pharisees had not gone that far, but were living within Jerusalem, operating within the temple environment. They were encouraging purity in regard to the Law in order to please God and bring about His deliverance. In seeking purity, however, they had failed to maintain a witness to the Gentiles and saw them as enemies. On the other hand, there were the Sadducees and many others who had accepted the Greek influence and were forsaking their roots. Into this world Jesus shone a new kind of light, one that fulfilled the Old Testament Law in keeping with its original intent: to bring salvation to the nations. Jesus was the rock that would strike the feet of iron and clay and cause the statue to turn to dust; He was bringing in a new kind of kingdom.

Unit 1: The Incarnation of Christ

APPLICATION

Israel's failure to shine their light without making detrimental accommodations to the Greek culture provides a helpful analogy in regard to our call to be a light to the world without becoming "of" the world. People generally tend to one extreme or the other. Evaluate your heart to see which error you are prone to. Then find concrete steps towards balance and shining your light in a healthy way.

ACTIVITIES

1. Daniel's Statue. Read Daniel 2:31-35 and draw the statue that Nebuchadnezzar saw in his dream. Label each section of the statue with the appropriate kingdom.

2. Separation and Accommodation. During the time between the Old Testament and the New Testament, the Jewish people were exiled among foreign nations, and then later, lived in Israel under the rule of the Greeks and Romans. During this time, many Jews became just like the Greeks (accommodation). On the other hand, Jews who didn't want to become like the Greeks tended to completely separate themselves from Greek culture, creating their own isolated communities (separation). In both of these ways of relating to the world (accommodation and separation) they failed to properly shine the light into the Gentile world. The same temptations are present in the lives of all Christians today. Fill in the blanks in the following chart with how a Christian who is trying to separate from the world might behave in each of these areas of life. Do the same for the Christian who is trying to accommodate the world in each of these areas. Finally, fill in the blank for how a Christian should behave to shine the light without accommodating in each of these areas of life. Then, answer the questions on the following page.

Area of Life	Separation	Accommodation	Shine The Light
Music, movies, tv			
Relationships with unbelievers			
Sports			
Politics			

Unit 1: The Incarnation of Christ

Which temptation are you more attracted to: accommodation or separation? _____

_____

_____

What can you do to help protect yourself from that temptation? _____

_____

_____

_____

_____

_____

_____

_____

_____

EVALUATION

1. What do each of the different sections of the statue in Daniel 2 represent? _____

2. What does the rock not cut with hands represent out of Daniel 2? _____

3. Who were the Maccabees? _____

4. Who were the Hasmoneans and how were they connected with the Maccabees? _____

5. Who was Herod the Great, and in what way did he set the stage for the coming of the Messiah? _____

6. How did the world and Israel's relationship with it change after the return from exile? _____

7. How did Israel do at shining their light from within? _____

   In what ways did they fail? _____

LESSON 1.2

The New Creation

UNIT 1

NOTES TO THE TEACHER

Lesson Theme - The new creation

All things are made new; that is the point of this lesson. When Jesus came into the world, it was the beginning of a new creation, a new Genesis... and it changed *everything*. To recycle a metaphor from the apostle John, there aren't enough books in the world to contain all the ways Jesus changes everything; so we will narrow in on just three ways in this lesson. First, Jesus' incarnation changes the way we read Genesis 1. John 1:1-3 tells us the Son was there in the beginning, actively creating the world, and if we look closely at Genesis 1, we can find Him. Second, and following from the first, the incarnation changes the way we read the entire Old Testament. It turns out the Law, Prophets and Writings are *about* the Son. Finally, the incarnation affects the creation—in Genesis 1, the Word spoke the world into being; in John 1, the Word became flesh, part of the creation.

If we only had the Old Testament, it would be very difficult (or perhaps impossible) to develop a concept of the Trinity. Sure, the Spirit shows up a number of times, and Yahweh takes on flesh on occasion, but the details are sparse. However, armed with an understanding of John 1:1-3, Genesis 1:1-3 becomes 3D. John 1:1-2 tells us that the Word was both *with* God and *was* God, and with that simple pair of statements we are thrust into Trinitarian paradox. The fact that the Word was *with* God indicates that He and God are two, but also, He *was* God, indicating oneness. Returning to Genesis 1, we read in verse 1 that God (the Father) created the heavens and the earth, but He did it by His Word—He spoke

OVERVIEW

The incarnation of Jesus Christ changes *everything*. The incarnation changes the way believers read Genesis 1 and therefore, the entire Old Testament. Furthermore, the incarnation transforms the old creation to a new creation from the inside out.

SOURCE MATERIAL

- John 1:1-3, 14, 16-18
- Genesis 1:1-5
- 2 Corinthians 5:17
- Psalm 149
- *Rose Book of Bible Charts, Maps and Timelines*, pages 180-183

(Gen 1:3). There, in Genesis 1:3, we have the Son—the Word—taking part in creation, putting the Father's desires into action. Also, notice that the Holy Spirit is present as well in Genesis 1:2, hovering over the face of the waters.

This raises the question: if the Son was there in Genesis 1:3, where else in the Old Testament can we see Him? Furthermore, if the narrative of the Old Testament was heading toward the incarnation all along, what might we have missed along the way? The Messiah, the Son of God, stands behind every bit of story, every law, and every psalm and proverb in the Old Testament. He is the substance of which they were the shadow; He is the ultimate Priest, King and Prophet. He is the Lawgiver, Judge, Head-Crusher and obedient Son. If anything, the Old Testament leaves us

Unit 1: The Incarnation of Christ

OBJECTIVES

Feel...

- excited about the new creation and what it means for us.
- thankful that the Word became flesh.

Understand...

- that the incarnation changes the way we read Genesis 1.
- that the incarnation changes the way we read the Old Testament.
- that the incarnation transforms the old creation from the inside out into an entirely new creation.
- where the Spirit and the Son show up in Genesis 1:1-3.

Apply this understanding by...

- believing that transformation for sinners is possible.
- identifying any areas in your life where you don't believe God can change you and asking that He would.

hungry for more: a better king, a more faithful priest, a more powerful judge. The Son of God is there in that hunger and stands behind everything as the hope for a new creation in which the brokenness in the old is healed.

"And the Word became flesh" (John 1:14); this was the beginning of a new creation. But not a new creation somewhere else, a new creation *within* the old one. In Genesis 1, the Son speaks the creation into being; in John 1:1, He takes on flesh and becomes a part of creation, but not just another part. He is a part of creation like a seed is a part of the ground—new life to transform the old and dead.

APPLICATION

The fact that the Son took on flesh—entered into the old creation in order to transform it—is the theological basis for the hope that *we* as a part of the old creation can be transformed as well. Think about it: God became man to make it possible to break free from the curse and live in fellowship with God!

The application for this lesson is to believe that we can be transformed, even in areas where we have a history of failure. This is a truth you need to take home and walk in. The key verse for this application is 2 Corinthians 5:17, "Therefore, if anyone is in Christ, he is a new creation; old things have passed away; behold, all things have become new." You may have struggled long with the same sins; find hope with this truth: transformation is possible because God became man.

ADDITIONAL NOTES

We cannot read the New Testament without making constant reference to the Old. On nearly every page of the New Testament there are references, allusions, parallels and fulfillments of the Old Testament. Throughout this curriculum we will uncover and explore as many of these as possible; nearly every lesson in this curriculum will make reference to a pattern, prophecy or parallel that has been fulfilled. This will take some additional effort, but the work will be repaid with a rich and multifaceted understanding of our Lord and of the writings of the New Testament.

This curriculum depends heavily on the Old Testament curriculum. Many of the shadows of which we will see the substance in this curriculum will be drawn from Old Testament references in that curriculum.

Lesson 1.2

ACTIVITIES

1. Trinity Analogy Project. There are a number of common analogies that are used to try to explain how there can be only one God, yet three persons in the Trinity. All of these analogies ultimately fail and actually teach a false view of the Trinity. For each of the following analogies, write an explanation of what is wrong with the analogy in the space below it. Finally, invent your own analogy for the Trinity and explain where it goes wrong in explaining the Trinity.

False Analogy #1: God is like an egg. There is only one egg, but three parts: the shell, yolk and white. Likewise, God is made up of the Father, Son and Holy Spirit. What is wrong with this analogy?_____

_____
_____
_____
_____
_____

False Analogy #2: God is like water that exists in three different forms: solid (ice), liquid (water) and gas (water vapor). Likewise, God appears as three forms: Father, Son and Holy Spirit. What is wrong with this analogy?_____

_____
_____
_____

Write your own analogy:_____

_____
_____
_____

What is wrong with your own analogy?_____

_____
_____

Unit 1: The Incarnation of Christ

2. Journal Time: Transformation. The incarnation of Jesus Christ changes the old creation into an entirely new creation, from the inside out. The incarnation means that transformation for sinners is possible. Spend some time writing in the space below. Identify an area in your life where you need transformation and write out a prayer, asking God to transform even those areas you have the hardest time believing will ever change. _____

_____
_____
_____
_____
_____
_____

3. Psalm Singing Activity. Sing or read Psalm 149 and write a short prayer of thanksgiving to God in the space below. _____

_____
_____
_____
_____
_____
_____
_____
_____
_____
_____

Lesson 1.2

EVALUATION

1. What does John 1:1-3 tell us about Genesis 1:1-3? _____
_____
_____
_____

2. What does the fact that the Son was with God in the beginning tell us about the rest of the Old Testament? _____
_____
_____
_____

3. How does the incarnation impact all of creation? _____
_____
_____
_____

4. What does the incarnation mean for us as Christians?_____
_____
_____
_____

LESSON 1.3

The Seed-Line: The New Adam and Son of David

UNIT 1

NOTES TO THE TEACHER

Lesson Theme - Jesus is the promised Seed.
In Genesis 3:15 God promised that a seed (descendant) of the woman would crush the head of the serpent. Eve thought that perhaps Cain or Abel was the promised son, but it became clear that the promised son was not coming anytime soon. Instead, God was developing a line of descendants generation after generation made up of important patriarchs, kings and prophets who foreshadowed the coming Messiah. Jesus was the fulfillment of the seed-line and the fulfillment of the hopes of Israel and the people of the earth for a deliverer.

Both the books of Matthew and Luke record a genealogy of Jesus, and there are several important differences between these genealogies. First, they record the same genealogy between Abraham and David; but after David, Matthew traces the line through Solomon and the kings of Judah, while Luke traces the line through Solomon's brother Nathan. The reason for this difference is simple: Matthew traces the line through Jesus' adopted father Joseph, and Luke traces Mary's

OVERVIEW

Jesus is the culmination of the seed-line: the line of descendants promised to ultimately produce *a* Seed who would crush the head of the serpent. Jesus is the new Adam, the Son of Abraham and the promised Son of David. The hope that humanity will be redeemed from the fall rests on this promised Son for whom Israel had been waiting for many generations. Matthew and Luke both record a genealogy of Jesus Christ to prove that He had the proper lineage to be the Messiah.

SOURCE MATERIAL

- Matthew 1:1-17
- Luke 3:23-38
- Genesis 3:15
- Psalm 89
- *Rose Book of Bible Charts, Maps and Timelines*, page 80

Matthew's Genealogy	Luke's Genealogy
Abraham	Adam, Son of God
↓	↑
Jesus Christ	Jesus Christ

genealogy. Additionally, it is worth noticing that Matthew's genealogy starts from Abraham and works forward to Jesus Christ, while Luke's genealogy starts with Jesus and works backward to "... Son of Adam, Son of God" (Luke 3:38).

Matthew and Luke were writing to different audiences and were interested in making different points from their genealogies. Matthew was especially drawing attention to the fact that

Unit 1: The Incarnation of Christ

OBJECTIVES

Feel...

- joy and relief that the long awaited Seed-Son had finally come.
- anticipation to see how Jesus would fulfill the hopes of the patriarchs.

Understand...

- the similarities and differences between Luke's and Matthew's genealogies.
- that Luke was addressing Gentiles and therefore his genealogy shows that Jesus is the new Adam.
- that Matthew was addressing Jews, and his genealogy demonstrates Jesus' credentials as the Messiah (Son of Abraham, Son of David).
- that God is faithful, but sometimes takes a long time to fulfill His promises.

Apply this understanding by...

- resting in the hope that some promises won't be fulfilled in this life, but will be fulfilled hereafter.
- learning to wait patiently for the promises God will fulfill in this life.

Jesus was the fulfillment of the covenants made with Abraham and David. His gospel was directed at a Jewish audience, and he was interested in providing Jesus' Jewish credentials as Messiah. Luke was interested in the parallels and differences between Adam and Jesus, so he traced His genealogy all the way back. Jesus is the second Man, and He succeeded where Adam failed. In Matthew, Jesus is the new Israel, the Son of David.

God keeps His promises! He promised a deliverer would come through the seed of the woman, and when the deliverer came, He was everything He needed to be to deliver on God's promises.

APPLICATION

God is a promise maker and a promise keeper. Israel had waited literally thousands of years for God to make good on His promise in Genesis 3:15, and He did! The lesson for us is twofold—God always keeps His promises, and sometimes we have to wait a long time for it. Imagine Abraham: God promised him a seed who would rule over a kingdom that would never end. Not only was that promise not fulfilled in Abraham's lifetime; it wasn't fulfilled for another 42 generations!

This leads to two practical lessons. First, our ultimate hope will not be fulfilled in this lifetime, and that's okay, for we are not of this world. Second, we need to wait patiently, even for the promises that will be fulfilled in our lifetime.

Lesson 1.3

ACTIVITIES

1. Construct the Genealogy. Matthew and Luke both record genealogies for Jesus. The genealogy according to Matthew is written below. Break the genealogy up according to the following passages, labeling each section with the appropriate passage where the genealogical record is recorded in the Old Testament. After Zerubbabel, the names were taken from Joseph's family records and are not recorded in the Old Testament. Use the following Old Testament passages for this assignment: Genesis 25:19, 26, 35:22-26, 38:29; Ruth 4:18-22; 1 Chronicles 3:1-17.

Abraham	Obed	Jotham	Azor
Isaac	Jesse	Ahaz	Zadok
Jacob	David & wife of Uriah	Hezekiah	Achim
Judah & Tamar		Manasseh	Eliud
Perez	Solomon	Amon	Eleazar
Hezron	Rehoboam	Josiah	Matthan
Ram	Abijam	Jeconiah	Jacob
Amminadab	Asa	Shealtiel	Joseph & Mary
Nahshon	Jehoshaphat	Zerubbabel	Jesus
Salmon & Rahab	Jehoram	Abiud	
Boaz & Ruth	Uzziah	Eliakim	

2. My Family Tree. Our culture doesn't value genealogies as much as Jesus' culture did or even other modern-day cultures do. A genealogy or family tree and the family history that accompanies it can provide a source of identity; when we know our family history, we know that we belong within a greater story. Make a family tree going back three generations (to your great-grandparents). In addition to finding names of people, try to find stories of your ancestors. (As with any family, your family is made of human sinners, so not all of the stories you discover will be good ones.)

Unit 1: The Incarnation of Christ

_____
(me)

_____   _____
(my dad)   (my mom)

_____   _____   _____   _____
(dad's dad)   (dad's mom)   (mom's dad)   (mom's mom)

____ ____ ____ ____ ____ ____ ____ ____
(great (great (great (great (great (great (great (great
grandpa) grandma) grandpa) grandma) grandpa) grandma) grandpa) grandma)

After making your family tree, write out one of your favorite stories and what it means to you, in the space below._____

_____
_____
_____
_____
_____
_____
_____
_____
_____
_____
_____
_____
_____
_____
_____

Lesson 1.3

EVALUATION

1. What are the main differences between Luke's and Matthew's genealogies? _____
_____
_____
_____

2. Why does Luke's genealogy end at Adam? _____
_____

3. Why does Matthew's start at Abraham? _____
_____

4. Why is it important to have a record of Jesus' ancestry?_____
_____
_____

LESSON 1.4

Miraculous Births: John and Jesus

UNIT 1

NOTES TO THE TEACHER

Lesson Theme - Double miraculous births foretell redemption.

Throughout the Old Testament there is a repeated pattern of miraculous births. Whenever God was getting ready to do something awesome, bring about some great and miraculous deliverance, He would cause a barren woman to get pregnant, and the miraculous conception would bring a deliverer into the world. When the deliverance needed was especially important and called for a greater display of God's power, He would cause two miraculous births. In this lesson we see two miraculous births: one forerunner born to a barren woman, followed by the Messiah born to a virgin. The first birth revealed that God was getting ready to do something great; the second birth announced a new creation.

We will focus on Luke's presentation of the birth narratives of John and Jesus through the Old Testament lens of the stories of Samson and Samuel. Luke makes several clear allusions to Jesus as a new Samuel, and though it doesn't come across as clearly, the parallels indicate that John the Baptist is a parallel figure to Samson. Though their stories are not told together, chronologically we can deduce that Samson and Samuel were both born around the same time and both worked to deliver Israel from servitude to the Philistines.

Both Samson and John the Baptist were miraculously born to barren women whose births were accompanied by an angelic announcement di-

OVERVIEW

Much like the period of the Judges when Israel was oppressed by the Philistines and a host of Canaanites, during the time of Jesus' birth, Israel was under the oppression of a variety of evil forces (demons, disease, wicked religious leaders and Roman overlords). During the period of the Judges, God caused not just one, but two miraculous births to bring about the deliverance of His people: Samson and Samuel were both born to barren women at the same time. Now again, God used two miraculous births to deliver His people. Both births were announced by angels, and while Mary received the news with faith, Zechariah did not.

SOURCE MATERIAL

- **Luke 1:1-2:40**
- Matthew 1:18-2:12
- 1 Samuel 1:1-2:11
- Judges 13:1-25

recting that they should be lifelong Nazarites (explained below). Both operated as independent judges of sorts and both prepared for the coming of a deliverance. Samson's battles with the Philistines prepared for Samuel to arrange the final battle that defeated the Philistines, while John the Baptist prepared the way for Jesus to deliver Israel from evil, sin and death. See OT Lesson 7.3 for a closer look at Samson.

Unit 1: The Incarnation of Christ

OBJECTIVES

Feel...

- joy that God sent a forerunner and a deliverer to redeem His people.
- anticipation to look at what John and Jesus did through the lens of the Old Testament parallels to Samson and Samuel.

Understand...

- the significance of two miraculous births at the same time.
- the parallels between Samson and John the Baptist and Samuel and Jesus.
- the parallels between Hannah and Mary (especially their songs).
- the Old Testament background behind, "Blessed are you among women" (Luke 1:42).
- why John the Baptist's birth called for so much rejoicing and Jesus' birth called for even more.
- the contrast between Zechariah's doubtful response and Mary's faithful response.

Apply this understanding by...

- evaluating your life to see if you have quick faith and an ability to rejoice like Mary or if you are prone to doubt like Zechariah.
- thanking God for areas in your life where you are quick to believe and repenting in areas where you are prone to doubt.

The Nazirite vow was normally a temporary vow of dedication to the Lord to perform a particular task. During their vow, while they completed their task, they were not to cut their hair. Then, to complete their vow time, they would go to the temple and offer certain sacrifices, *including their hair*. That's right, when the task was done, they would offer their work back to God by offering their hair on the altar. Additionally, during the time of their vow, they were to show dedication to the Lord by not drinking any alcohol (wine or beer) or eating any grapes, and they had to stay away from unclean things and dead bodies.

There are a number of parallels between Jesus' birth narrative and Samuel's that indicate that Jesus is the new Samuel. Furthermore, Luke makes a clear allusion to 1 Samuel 1:26 in Luke 2:52 to indicate that he is intentionally setting up those links. Both Samuel's mother, Hannah, and Jesus' mother, Mary, wrote songs in celebration of their sons' miraculous births. In fact, many of the themes in the *Magnificat* (Mary's song) are drawn from Hannah's song (Luke 1:46-55 and 1 Sam 2:1-10). Furthermore, Mary and Hannah both referred to themselves as servants (Luke 1:38 and 1 Sam 1:18) and both were "favored" (Luke 1:28 and 1 Sam 1:18). Mary is a new Hannah.

In addition to this, Luke includes the story of the prophetess Anna who prayed at the temple and greeted Mary and Joseph with excitement about the coming redemption. Hannah and Anna share essentially the same name (the former Hebrew and the latter Greek—both meaning "favor"). Hannah prayed faithfully in the temple as Anna later did, and both received a word from the Lord about the coming child.

The story
The story begins with the announcement of John the Baptist's birth to Zechariah. As a priest, Zechariah was periodically on duty at the temple. During his duty, he was selected by lot to enter

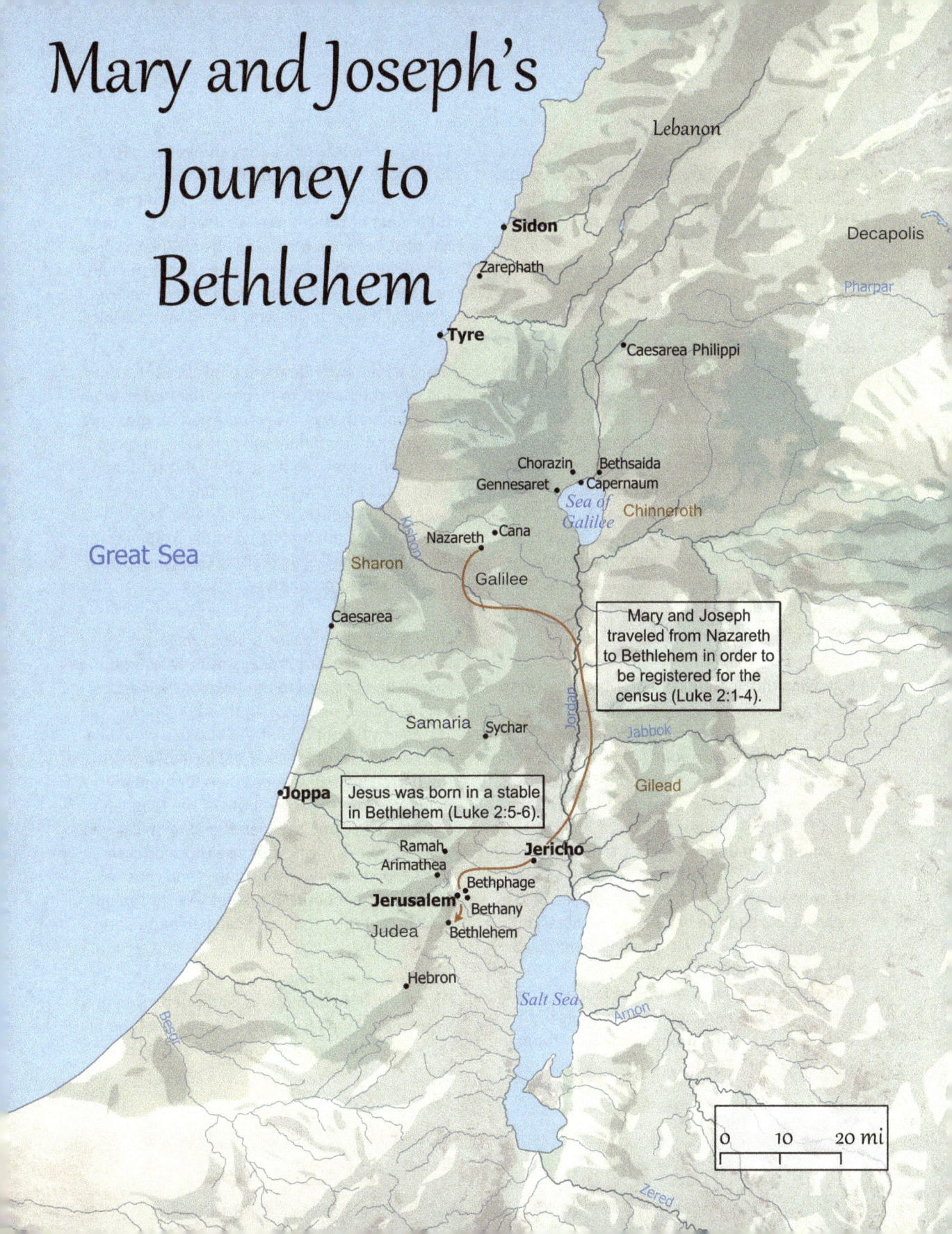

Unit 1: The Incarnation of Christ

the Holy Place to burn incense before the Lord (Luke 1:8). While there, an angel appeared to him and announced the upcoming miraculous birth of his son and explained his son's calling (Luke 1:11-17). Because he didn't immediately believe the promise of a son, the angel silenced Zechariah until John's birth (Luke 1:20).

Six months later, the angel Gabriel appeared to Mary and announced the coming of her son (Luke 1:26-27). Unlike the birth of John to a married, but barren woman (like Isaac's, Samson's, Samuel's births, etc), there is no precedent in the Old Testament for a birth to a virgin. So Mary asked how this was going to happen. The angel explained that the Holy Spirit was going to cause her pregnancy and assured her by telling her that her barren relative Elizabeth was pregnant as well. Mary responded with immediate faith and said, "I am the Lord's servant... may your word to me be fulfilled" (Luke 1:38, NIV).

Following this announcement, Mary hurried to visit Elizabeth who, along with the son in her womb, was excited to see Mary and announced with joy, "Blessed are you among women, and blessed is the fruit of your womb!" (Luke 1:42). Elizabeth was making reference to Deborah's song (Judg 5:24) where Jael was said to be blessed among women for driving a tent peg through the wicked Sisera. Mary was striking a blow to the serpent's head (in fulfillment of Gen 3:15) by giving birth to the head-crushing Messiah. Elizabeth and Mary are the new Deborah and Jael—head-crushing women. Like in the story of Deborah and Jael in the book of Judges, women are the central characters and heroines of this story, while the men dropped the ball (compare Zechariah and Barak).

Mary responded with a song that reflects Hannah's song (Luke 1:46-55). It emphasizes God's favor to the humble and oppressed and the fulfillment of His promises to Israel. Notice the contrast between Mary singing and Zechariah, who *couldn't* sing while he awaited the miraculous birth of his son, because he didn't believe. Unbelief always takes away our ability to rejoice.

Mary stayed with Elizabeth until about the time for John the Baptist to be born. The barren woman giving birth was always occasion for great joy, and so all of her family and neighbors rejoiced when John was born (Luke 1:58). But still, Zechariah was unable to join in the rejoicing on account of his silence. It wasn't until he confirmed the name of John that he was able to speak, and immediately he began praising God (Luke 1:64). He then began prophesying in song.

Not long after John's birth, Jesus was born. In order to take part in the census, Mary and Joseph had to travel to the town of their ancestors, Bethlehem (Luke 2:4), thus fulfilling the Old Testament prophecy that the Messiah would be born in the city of David. If the birth of a son to the barren woman was occasion for great joy, how much more was the birth of the Messiah to a virgin. It was not just friends and relatives who joined in the rejoicing, but also those as exalted as the heavenly host of angels and those as humble as shepherds in the field. Word spread quickly that the promised Seed had been born.

Jesus was dedicated at the temple according to custom, and His calling was confirmed again by Simeon and Anna (Luke 2:25-38). Both of them responded with joy and gratitude to the Lord.

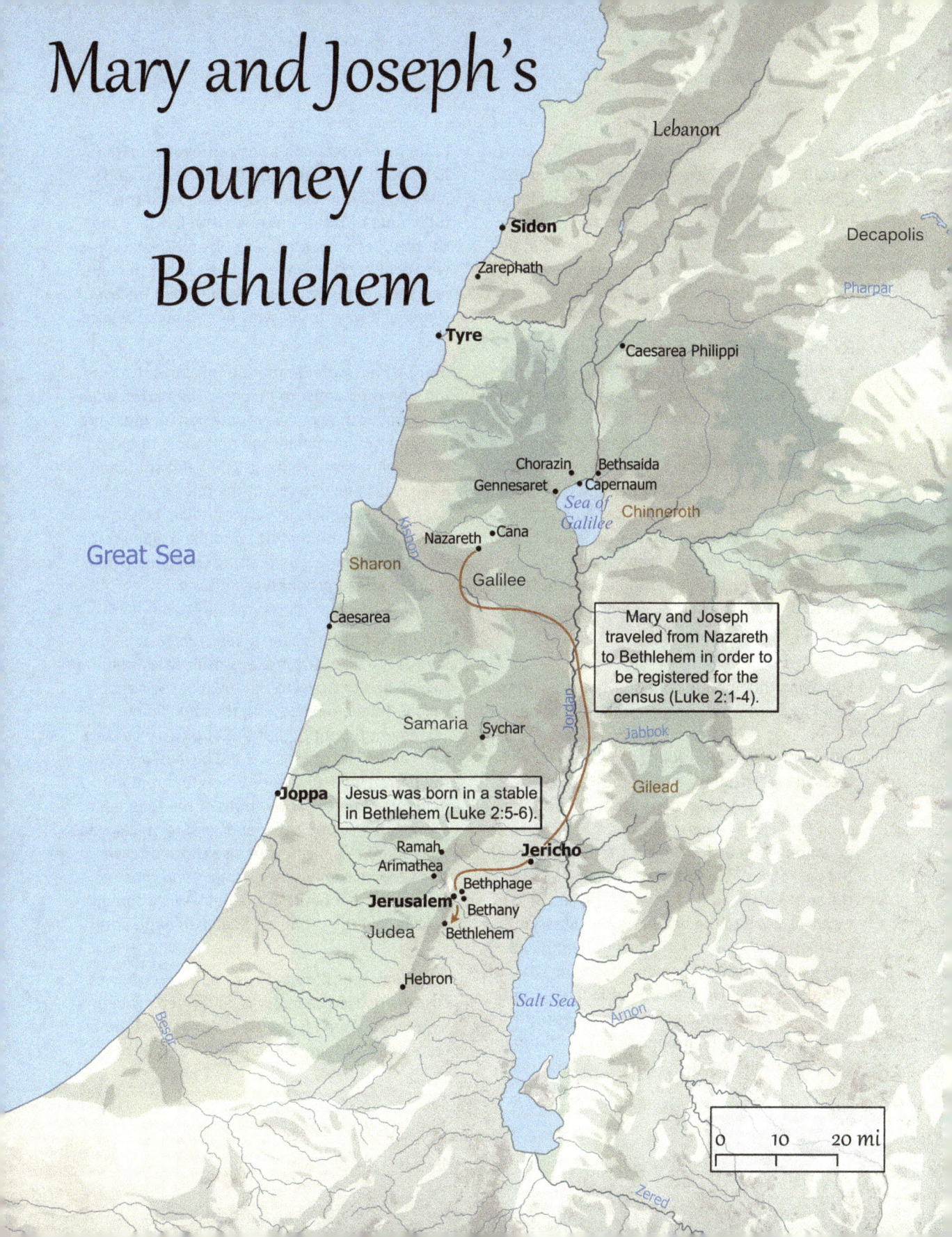

Unit 1: The Incarnation of Christ

the Holy Place to burn incense before the Lord (Luke 1:8). While there, an angel appeared to him and announced the upcoming miraculous birth of his son and explained his son's calling (Luke 1:11-17). Because he didn't immediately believe the promise of a son, the angel silenced Zechariah until John's birth (Luke 1:20).

Six months later, the angel Gabriel appeared to Mary and announced the coming of her son (Luke 1:26-27). Unlike the birth of John to a married, but barren woman (like Isaac's, Samson's, Samuel's births, etc), there is no precedent in the Old Testament for a birth to a virgin. So Mary asked how this was going to happen. The angel explained that the Holy Spirit was going to cause her pregnancy and assured her by telling her that her barren relative Elizabeth was pregnant as well. Mary responded with immediate faith and said, "I am the Lord's servant... may your word to me be fulfilled" (Luke 1:38, NIV).

Following this announcement, Mary hurried to visit Elizabeth who, along with the son in her womb, was excited to see Mary and announced with joy, "Blessed are you among women, and blessed is the fruit of your womb!" (Luke 1:42). Elizabeth was making reference to Deborah's song (Judg 5:24) where Jael was said to be blessed among women for driving a tent peg through the wicked Sisera. Mary was striking a blow to the serpent's head (in fulfillment of Gen 3:15) by giving birth to the head-crushing Messiah. Elizabeth and Mary are the new Deborah and Jael—head-crushing women. Like in the story of Deborah and Jael in the book of Judges, women are the central characters and heroines of this story, while the men dropped the ball (compare Zechariah and Barak).

Mary responded with a song that reflects Hannah's song (Luke 1:46-55). It emphasizes God's favor to the humble and oppressed and the fulfillment of His promises to Israel. Notice the contrast between Mary singing and Zechariah, who *couldn't* sing while he awaited the miraculous birth of his son, because he didn't believe. Unbelief always takes away our ability to rejoice.

Mary stayed with Elizabeth until about the time for John the Baptist to be born. The barren woman giving birth was always occasion for great joy, and so all of her family and neighbors rejoiced when John was born (Luke 1:58). But still, Zechariah was unable to join in the rejoicing on account of his silence. It wasn't until he confirmed the name of John that he was able to speak, and immediately he began praising God (Luke 1:64). He then began prophesying in song.

Not long after John's birth, Jesus was born. In order to take part in the census, Mary and Joseph had to travel to the town of their ancestors, Bethlehem (Luke 2:4), thus fulfilling the Old Testament prophecy that the Messiah would be born in the city of David. If the birth of a son to the barren woman was occasion for great joy, how much more was the birth of the Messiah to a virgin. It was not just friends and relatives who joined in the rejoicing, but also those as exalted as the heavenly host of angels and those as humble as shepherds in the field. Word spread quickly that the promised Seed had been born.

Jesus was dedicated at the temple according to custom, and His calling was confirmed again by Simeon and Anna (Luke 2:25-38). Both of them responded with joy and gratitude to the Lord.

Unit 1: The Incarnation of Christ

APPLICATION

Zechariah responded to the angels' announcement of John's birth with doubt, and he was struck with silence for the course of Elizabeth's pregnancy. Therefore, he wasn't able to join in the rejoicing either before or immediately after his son's birth. Mary immediately expressed her faith and was able to rejoice all along.

Doubt always inhibits our ability to rejoice and praise God for the good things He is doing. God's word is full of promises and hope, but if we don't receive those promises with faith, we are struck with the worst kind of silence: the ability to make noise but not rejoice. When we doubt, our joy is replaced with complaining or bitter speech; this is a worse punishment than Zechariah's. This point could be particularly applicable if you have a habit of complaining; when you lack faith, you only see the bad and rob yourself of joy.

ACTIVITIES

1. Faith and Joy, Doubt and Bitterness. In order to understand the connections between faith and joy and between doubt and bitterness, answer the following questions, based on Luke 1:1-2:40. Be prepared to discuss your answers.

What happened to Zechariah as a result of his doubt? _____

_____

_____

What do you think it was like for Zechariah to be unable to speak? _____

_____

What was Mary able to do right away because of her faith? _____

_____

This story teaches us that faith in God's promises leads to rejoicing, but doubt leads to an inability to praise God. When we doubt Him, God doesn't usually take away our ability to speak. Instead, doubt leads to something worse than silence—the ability to make noise but not rejoice. What are some examples of this type of noise? _____

_____

_____

Lesson 1.4

What's an example of a time in your life when you have noticed either how faith has led to joy or how doubt has led to a lack of joy? _____

_____

_____

_____

EVALUATION

1. What is the Old Testament significance of a barren woman getting pregnant? _____

_____

2. What is the significance of both a virgin and a barren woman bearing a son? _____

_____

3. What is the significance of two miraculous conceptions at about the same time? _____

_____

4. What do Samson and John the Baptist have in common? _____

_____

_____

5. What do Jesus and Samuel have in common? _____

_____

_____

6. Why did Elizabeth call Mary "Most blessed among women" (Luke 1:42)? _____

_____

7. What were the different responses to the angelic announcement for Zechariah and Mary? _____

_____

_____

8. What did Zechariah's doubt cost him? _____

_____

_____

LESSON 1.5

Jesus' Flight to Egypt: Jesus is the New Israel

UNIT 1

NOTES TO THE TEACHER

Lesson Theme - Jesus is the new Israel.
This lesson tells the story of a king who killed the children of the Israelite women, a story in which Jesus made an exodus to Egypt and a return to the land. Jesus is the new Israel who walked in the footsteps of Israel, succeeding where they had failed.

About two years after the birth of Jesus, Magi from the east arrived in Jerusalem seeking the newborn King whose star they had followed. We don't have much of a backstory on the Magi; and it is not the aim of this lesson to hypothesize where they came from, how many there might have been or what kind of star they were following. Rather than spending much time on these questions, help your students see that the birth of the Messiah was big news to *Gentiles;* the coming of the Messiah meant redemption for all mankind. Furthermore, God saw fit to tell some Gentiles of His coming and invite them to visit their newborn King.

The Magi went to Jerusalem to speak to Herod about this new King whom they had come to visit. Herod was a shrewd and power hungry politician. He had fought hard to gain power over Israel and won the title "King of the Jews" from Caesar. So when the Magi showed up and said, "Where is He who has been born King of the Jews? For we have seen His star in the East and have come to worship Him" (Matt 2:2), Herod was greatly threatened.

Here it gets interesting. Herod sent for the priests and teachers of the law to help answer

OVERVIEW

Herod had heard from the Magi that there was a king born in Bethlehem. He was hoping to find out from the Magi who this king was so he could kill Him to secure his throne. The Magi, however, outwitted him and returned to their land by a different route. Herod became angry and gave orders to kill all the boys two years of age and under. An angel warned Joseph, so Jesus' family fled to Egypt where they remained until Herod died. Joseph and his family then returned to Israel and raised Jesus in Nazareth. Throughout this lesson, we see parallels between Jesus and the period of Israel's exodus; Jesus is the new Israel.

SOURCE MATERIAL

- Matthew 2:1-23
- Exodus 1

the Magi's question. He apparently believed the Old Testament prophecy that the Messiah would be born in Bethlehem (Mic 5:2,4), but thought he could beat God. (Remember, Herod was the self-exalting king spoken of in Daniel 11; see Lesson 1.1). This "King of the Jews" really did think he was exalted as high as God. So he told the Magi to find the newborn King and report back to him so that he could go worship Him too. However, Herod's real plan was to go kill Him to protect his throne.

After visiting the Messiah, the Magi were warned in a dream not to go back to Herod, so they

Unit 1: The Incarnation of Christ

OBJECTIVES

Feel...

- joy that the Gentiles were excited about the coming of the King.
- thankful that God was so carefully orchestrating the story.
    - God used angels to direct Joseph and the Magi.
    - God painted a picture that Jesus is the new Israel.

Understand...

- that Herod was threatened by the possibility of a promised King.
- that Herod thought he could "beat" God.
- the parallels between Jesus' flight to Egypt and Israel's exodus.
    - Jesus is the new Israel.
    - Herod was a new Pharaoh.
    - Israel was a new Egypt that Jesus fled from.
    - Jesus is the new Moses returning to deliver His people.
- that the coming of the Messiah was good news to *Gentiles*, not only Jews.

Apply this understanding by...

- comparing your desire to worship the Lord to the Magi's.

traveled home by another route. When Herod learned that the Magi had tricked him, he gave orders to kill all boys two years and under in and around Bethlehem since the Magi had told him that the star had shown up two years before. This caused great suffering in Bethlehem. However, the angel of the Lord had appeared to Joseph and told him to flee to Egypt, so Herod was not able to kill God's Messiah.

In this passage, we see a number of parallels to Israel in Egypt, Moses, and the exodus, but it is not neat and tidy. The parallels are out of sequence and multi-faceted. This is how Old Testament typology works.

Herod was a new Pharaoh and Israel was a new Egypt. Like Herod, Pharaoh had all of the Israelite boys killed (Exod 1:22) to protect his rule (Exod 1:9). Joseph and his family went *to* Egypt to escape from this new Pharaoh. Matthew tells us that this all happened to fulfill Hosea 11:1—"Out of Egypt I called My son"—which was written about Israel, not Jesus (directly): Jesus is the new Israel.

After Herod died, an angel of the Lord appeared to Joseph to tell him that it was safe to return to Israel since "those who sought the young Child's life are dead" (Matt 2:20). These words are almost identical to God's words to Moses after his time in the desert with the Midianites: "Go, return to Egypt; for all the men who sought your life are dead" (Exod 4:19). Jesus is the new Moses going back to free the Israelites from slavery.

This lesson taken together with Lessons 2.2 and 2.3 paints a broader picture of Jesus as the new Israel. In this lesson, Jesus journeys from Egypt to Israel. After His return, He was baptized in the Jordan like Israel was baptized in the Red Sea, and then was tested in the wilderness for 40 days like Israel was tested for 40 years.

Lesson 1.5

APPLICATION

Take some time to reflect on what the Magi did. Before there were cars or planes, they traveled a very long distance. They brought extremely expensive gifts to *a child*, and they sat at His feet and worshiped Him. They showed profound faith, incredible generosity and a deeply burning desire to worship the Lord.

Now reflect on your own life. Do you desire to worship the Lord anywhere near that much? In all likelihood the answer is no; on the one hand, that's not okay. On the other hand, the point of this activity isn't to make you feel guilty, but to capture your imagination. Your heart should respond by saying, "If Jesus is that worthy of worship, what am I missing out on?" Pray that your desire to worship the Lord would grow.

ACTIVITIES

1. Count the Cost. Calculate how much the gifts of gold, frankincense and myrrh were worth in the first century, but calculated in today's dollars. We don't know exactly how much the magi brought to Jesus, but just assume a fairly small amount of each, perhaps 1 pound. Use Internet sources to try to calculate the cost as best you can.

Value of one pound of gold in the first century (in today's dollars): $_____

Value of one pound of frankincense in the first century (in today's dollars): $_____

Value of one pound of myrrh in the first century (in today's dollars): $_____

Total Value: $_____

Unit 1: The Incarnation of Christ

2. Journal Time: The Magi's Sacrifice. Spend some time thinking about all the sacrifices the Magi made in order to come worship a child. They traveled a very long distance, gave him very expensive gifts, and provoked the wrath of King Herod by not obeying his command to tell him who the child was. They risked so much, just so they could worship Jesus, because they knew what the arrival of this child meant for them. They showed profound faith, incredible generosity and a deeply burning desire to worship the Lord. Reflect on your own life, then write about the following in your journal or the space below.

Do you desire to worship the Lord anywhere near as much as the Magi did?_____

_____
_____
_____
_____

What sacrifices have you had to make or have been unwilling to make in order to worship the Lord?___

_____
_____
_____
_____

The Magi were willing to sacrifice their time, money, comfort and safety in order to worship Jesus, because they understood how important He is. Pray that God would open your eyes to see what you are missing out on by not worshipping Jesus with your whole heart. Pray that your desire to worship the Lord would grow. Write a short prayer in the space below._____

_____
_____
_____
_____
_____
_____

Lesson 1.5

EVALUATION

1. What is significant about the Magi coming from a foreign land? _____
_____
_____

2. Why was Herod so threatened by the baby King in Bethlehem? _____
_____
_____
_____

3. What Old Testament character was Herod similar to? _____
_____
_____

4. In what way is Jesus the new Israel? _____
_____
_____

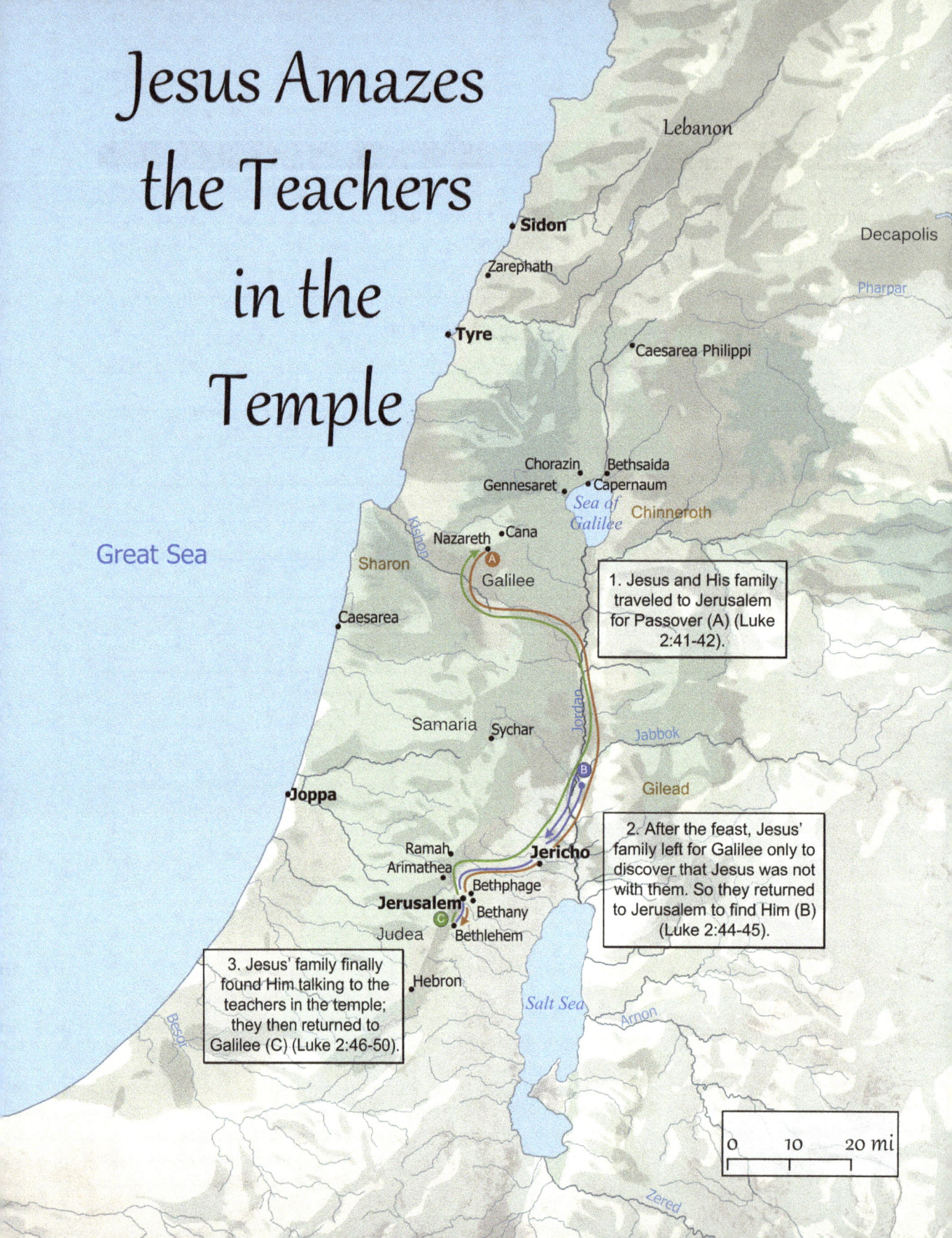

LESSON 1.6

The Foreshadowing of Jesus' Temple Ministry

UNIT 1

NOTES TO THE TEACHER

Lesson Theme - Jesus, the Son of God, came to supplant the wicked priests in God's house. Joseph was not Jesus' father as some thought; God above was His Father. As such, His ultimate home was not Joseph's house, but His heavenly Father's house—the temple. In this lesson, the 12-year-old Jesus foreshadows His later ministry by questioning and answering the priests in the temple. He showed that He was indeed the new Samuel; a prophet who would supplant the corrupt priests.

In Lesson 1.4 we saw that Luke makes a number of intentional parallels with 1 Samuel to indicate that Jesus is a new and greater Samuel. In this lesson, we see that theme reinforced and begin to see in exactly what way Jesus fulfilled Samuel's ministry.

Samuel was not from the tribe of Levi, so he had no official credentials as a priest. However, he was dedicated to the Lord from birth, so he grew up in the temple and was trained by Eli, the high priest. Eli's line had been chosen by God from the time Israel was in slavery in Egypt (1 Sam 2:27-28); but Eli's sons were wicked, and Eli was held accountable for allowing them to desecrate things sanctified to the Lord (1 Sam 2:12-25). Because of their wickedness, God said that Eli's line would be rejected and his sons would both die on the same day.

Throughout this narrative, Samuel is contrasted with Eli's sons as being a faithful prophet in the house of God. Even as a boy, he faithfully minis-

OVERVIEW

Samuel was the prophet called to supplant the wicked priests, and Jesus is the new Samuel. Even as a 12-year-old, Jesus spent time in His true Father's house, questioning and answering the priests. This story foreshadows His later questioning of the priests in the temple. This questioning would ultimately lead to His arrest, death and resurrection upon which He would ascend to His Father's right hand and supplant the wicked priests.

SOURCE MATERIAL

- Luke 2:41-52
- 1 Samuel 1-2
- Proverbs 1:8

tered before the Lord under Eli. On one occasion, the Lord appeared to Samuel to tell Him that He had rejected Eli's line (1 Sam 3:1-14). From that time on Samuel would regularly hear from the Lord and spoke as a prophet before Eli and all of Israel.

In time, God fulfilled His words, and the sons of Eli were killed. Immediately afterward, Eli died as well. Additionally, the ark was captured and carried off by the Philistines. In all likelihood, Shiloh (the location of the tabernacle during that time) was sacked. So Israel was left without a priestly line and without a place of worship. Later in 1 Samuel, we see that Samuel was responsible for

Unit 1: The Incarnation of Christ

OBJECTIVES

Feel...

- excited that Jesus was already fulfilling His calling in a preliminary way at the age of 12.
- impressed with the importance God places on the young even if it is just preparation for their future calling.

Understand...

- that Jesus' home was in His heavenly Father's house.
- that Jesus is a new and greater Samuel.
- what Jesus' interaction with the priests foreshadows about His later ministry in the temple.
- that, like Samuel, Jesus was a prophet who would supplant the wicked priests.
- that, like Samuel, Jesus showed great maturity at a young age.

Apply this understanding by...

- valuing faithfulness to God at any age.

offering sacrifices; the righteous prophet had supplanted the wicked priests.

Like Samuel, Jesus spent time as a young boy in the temple, interacting with the priests even though He was not of the tribe of Levi. Like Samuel, Jesus "increased in wisdom and stature, and in favor with God and men" (Luke 2:52, 1 Sam 2:26). And like Samuel, Jesus would ultimately be the prophet who would supplant the wicked priests.

This short story of Jesus in the temple as a 12-year-old foreshadows His interactions with the priests in His later ministry. He was both questioning and answering the priests (Luke 2:46-47) in His Father's house. Later, His questioning and answering of the priests would lead to His arrest (Luke 20-22). Ultimately, like Samuel, He was the prophet who supplanted the priests when He ascended to the right hand of God.

Another angle to take on this passage is to see it as a coming of age story. There comes a day when every child must leave his parents and move away. This should not be a rejection of one's father, or (worse) a rejection of fatherhood. Rather, maturity comes when a child leaves his earthly father and grows into a relationship with God as his heavenly Father. In this lesson, Jesus leaves His earthly father to live in His heavenly Father's house. Proverbs 1:8 says, "My son, hear the instruction of your father, and do not forsake the law of your mother." Growing up happens when you leave your father and mother without rejecting their instruction—coming under the fatherhood of God.

The Old Testament has a number of coming of age stories. The pattern of these stories is that the son would leave his father and come of age in a foreign land. Normally, the son would find a new father in the foreign land, whether good or bad. Jacob came under Laban, Judah exchanged his family for Canaanites, and Joseph grew into a relationship with God in Egypt. See OT Lessons 3.7 and 4.3 for the Old Testament background to this theme.

Unit 1: The Incarnation of Christ

APPLICATION

You are becoming now what you will be. Where will you end up if you continue on the path you are currently on? Jesus, at 12 years of age, was already becoming the kind of person who could interact with the priests at the temple, challenging them and answering their questions. It might be easy to think that what you think and do doesn't matter that much. This is a lie from our culture and from Satan. There is often a chance to repent, but the sooner you start on the path of the wise, the further along you will get.

ACTIVITIES

1. Compare Jesus to Samuel. Read 1 Samuel 1-2 and Luke 2:41-52 and, on the next page, make a list of as many similarities between Samuel and Jesus as young men. Use your creativity; it doesn't have to be an exact similarity to make it onto the list, just find as many as you can.

Samuel	Jesus

Lesson 1.6

2. Journal Time: 12-Year-Old Jesus. As a 12-year-old, Jesus was already becoming who He would be when He was grown up. Think through your past. What decisions did you make that put you on the right or wrong path? _____
_____
_____
_____
_____

Where is your current path leading? Are there any changes you need to make to get on the path of the wise? _____
_____
_____
_____
_____
_____

EVALUATION

1. In what ways was Jesus like Samuel? _____
_____
_____
_____

2. What did Jesus' interaction with the priests tell us about His later ministry in the temple? _____
_____
_____
_____

3. Why was Jesus surprised that His parents were shocked that He was in the temple? _____
_____
_____
_____

UNIT 2: JESUS' MINISTRY BEGINS

John the Baptist prepared the way for Jesus' ministry by calling the nation to repentance and baptism—God was calling a new people for Himself out of the corrupt establishment in Israel. Jesus, having return from His exodus in Egypt, "crossed" the Jordan by being baptized by John. Jesus was the new Israel and the head of the new people John was constituting through baptism. The Spirit then led Jesus into the wilderness, where He fasted and was tempted as Adam and Eve were once tempted. Unlike them, Jesus passed the test with flying colors.

Following Jesus' baptism and temptation, John became less and Jesus became greater. Shortly thereafter, John was imprisoned and killed by Herod, while Jesus performed miracles and preached the gospel throughout Israel. But John will always be remembered for making much of Jesus.

Jesus' ministry was the beginning of the new creation. Throughout the Bible, wine is associated with new creations, so it was appropriate that Jesus would reveal His glory at a wedding feast by turning ceremonial water into wine—the New Covenant was a covenant of celebration.

Shortly thereafter, Jesus' ministry began in earnest, first in Jerusalem, then in Samaria. At the Passover feast in Jerusalem, He cast the money changers out of the temple, preached the gospel and performed miracles. Many in Jerusalem believed in Him, but He would not entrust himself to them. After leaving Jerusalem, Jesus and His closest followers went through Samaria. While there, Jesus met a Samaritan woman at Jacob's well and offered her living water. After a brief conversation with Jesus, she believed and went to tell her whole town about the man she met at the well.

LESSON 2.1

The Ministry of John the Baptist

UNIT 2

NOTES TO THE TEACHER

Lesson Theme - John re-created God's people through baptism.
This lesson focuses on the symbolism of John's ministry. Of course, John was preparing the way for the Messiah, but *how* he went about it was crucial.

John is known as "John the Baptist" or "John the Baptizer" for a reason. He did no miracles; he was not like the Old Testament prophets in that sense. What he did do was preach and baptize, and it is important to note that every time he baptized, he was out in the Judean wilderness.

Look at John 1:19-28. Notice the questions the religious leaders asked John. They clearly expected him to claim to be the Messiah, but he told them he was not. Then they asked him if he was Elijah, because the Jews expected Elijah to come back and looked forward to his coming. He answered no there, too. Then they asked him if he was the Prophet, that is, the Prophet whom Moses foretold in Deuteronomy 18:15. And again, John replied no. At this point the religious leaders were out of ideas, and they simply had to ask him whom he claimed to be. John responded by quoting Isaiah 40:3. We'll come back to his answer, but before we talk about that, notice how the leaders responded to him, "Why then do you baptize if you are not the Christ, nor Elijah, nor the Prophet?" (John 1:25).

In modern Christian culture, we don't think of baptism this way, but in the culture of the time, it had tremendous significance. Since John was

OVERVIEW

While Jesus had come of age, John the Baptist had also come of age, and God led him out into the wilderness where he began to preach that the nation must prepare for the coming Messiah. By the way he conducted his ministry, John painted a picture: out of the corrupt establishment in Israel, God was calling a new people for Himself.

SOURCE MATERIAL

- **John 1:6-34**
- Matthew 3:1-11
- Mark 1:1-8
- Luke 3:1-19

baptizing, the religious leaders expected him to claim to be someone with *huge* authority—so much authority, in fact, that the only people they could think of who might have had enough were the Messiah, Elijah returned, or the Prophet like Moses.

So John's answer, "I am 'The voice of one crying in the wilderness'" (John 1:23), didn't compute for the religious leaders. In their eyes, he was admitting to be a *nobody*. He was just a guy going around saying, "God is coming; get ready!" In first-century Israel, people like that were as common as nuts on an almond tree. Taking that status might have justified John's preaching ministry; after all, there were many rabbis around, teaching and preaching, calling for repentance

Unit 2: Jesus' Ministry Begins

OBJECTIVES

Feel...

- the awkwardness of a nobody like John subverting the entire religious system by baptizing people.
- the boldness of being called by God to step up.

Understand...

- that John was a nobody in the eyes of the world, but he was faithful and bold.
- the symbolism of John's ministry.
    - Baptism implies being set apart by God for priestly work.
    - Baptism *in the wilderness* invokes the picture of Israel being brought out of Egypt and made a new nation.
    - Through John, God was calling a new chosen people out of Israel; in the process, John was also calling Israel the new Egypt, a place of slavery.

Apply this understanding by...

- considering what messages God might be calling you to speak out boldly.
- looking squarely at your excuses for being afraid instead of stepping out in faith to do what God has called you to do.
- overcoming your fears by emulating John's example of faithful boldness.

In order to understand the significance of baptism, imagine if you were a Jew like Zaccheus before John's ministry started. Like Zaccheus, you were a tax collector, and also like Zaccheus, a crooked one. But one day something happened and you repented. What would you do? Under the system of the time, you would go up to the temple, make the relevant sacrifices, and then make restitution.

John's ministry did something very different. Rather than sending the repentant person up to Jerusalem to the temple, John called the person *out into the wilderness to pass through water in baptism*. This was potent symbolism from Israel's history: God once called Israel out into the wilderness to be baptized in the Red Sea, which was the beginning of Israel's existence as an independent nation.

Understand that in Israel, ritual washing was very common. A great number of things could cause ritual impurity: contact with a dead body, most kinds of bodily discharges including the menstrual period and nocturnal emissions, sexual activity, and so on (see Lev 11, 15). The remedy for all these things was for the unclean person to wash himself and then wait until evening (when he would be purified by the evening sacrifice).

However, for all these ritual washings, the person would wash *himself*. Occasions when another person washed someone (i.e., a *baptism*) were very rare. God baptized the nation in the Red Sea, consecrating them as a nation of priests. Aaron and his sons were washed as part of the priestly ordination ceremony when they were consecrated as priests (see Exod 40:12ff). An ordinary Israelite would only need such a washing again if something happened that excluded him from the sacred congregation (like leprosy). A leper could not come into the temple and enter

and greater purity. None of this was particularly new or different, and none of it required the kind of authority the priests and Levites were expecting John to claim. Baptizing, though, was very different.

the presence of God; ritually, he was no longer a part of the priestly nation. If he was healed, the priests had to wash him before he could re-enter the temple. He was effectively being re-baptized, re-introduced into the priestly nation.

Baptism, for first-century Israel, had strong overtones of priestly ordination, of being chosen by God for special service. So John was not simply another hedge-preacher calling for the nation to repent and purify itself; that would have been tolerable to the Jewish leaders. No, John was baptizing in the wilderness; thus, he was painting a very specific picture, like Hosea painted a picture when he married Gomer (Hosea 1). The picture? *Israel had become the new Egypt, and out of it God was calling a new people for Himself. Come out into the wilderness and be baptized; become part of the new chosen people.*

For a nation that built its whole identity on being the chosen people, this claim was revolutionary; therefore, the religious leaders expected John to be claiming great authority.

APPLICATION

Throughout his ministry, John was an overwhelming example of humility. Imagine him at the beginning of his ministry. God appointed him to make the incredible claim that God was calling a new chosen people for Himself. Yet John was a nobody, and God gave him no credentials. Think of all the excuses he could have made: "God, I can't do this. I'm not a trained rabbi. I didn't go to school to learn theology. I'm not royalty. I'm not well-connected. I'm nobody. They're never going to listen to me; why should they? How can I go out there and make such a big claim?"

But John did make the big claim God called him to make, and he did it *boldly*. So should we. At a generic level, we can apply this attitude of boldness to the gospel: Jesus died to right *everything* that's wrong with the world. He paid for every sin, every dysfunction, every consequence of the fall on the cross, and He will do away with *all* that's wrong and make all things new in His kingdom. That's a *big* claim. We shouldn't be embarrassed to make it.

But more specifically, we shouldn't be embarrassed to do the specific things that bring little signs of His kingdom into people's lives right now. We pray, "Thy will be done on earth as it is in heaven," but do we mean it? Is bullying going on in heaven? No? Then we should stand up for the those being bullied here on earth! In heaven, do you think anybody is under-appreciated? No? Then how about you go find the least appreciated person at your place of work or school and tell him how much you appreciate his work. There are plenty more possibilities here, and a lot of them are so *weird* that we're embarrassed by them. Let's not be. John wasn't.

Unit 2: Jesus' Ministry Begins

ACTIVITIES

1. Being Bold. John the Baptist spoke boldly what God had called him to even though he was considered a nobody in Israel. Consider where God is calling you to be bold, to speak out about something. Maybe it's to oppose an oppressor; maybe it's to say "thank you" to someone who never gets thanked for his work. Maybe it's something else entirely. Brainstorm some things that God might be calling you to say and do that would require you to be a little uncomfortable; then write them in the column on the left. On the right side, across from each item on the left, write the reasons that you aren't currently doing these things. Put a star next to a couple of bold actions you want to do for God this week.

Bold things to do	Reasons why I'm not doing these things

2. John's Picture. When John was calling people to repent and be baptized, he was calling them to leave the bondage of Egypt (Israel) and be baptized in the Red Sea (baptism) so that God could make them into a new nation. God was calling out a new chosen people for Himself. Using the word bank following page, fill in the blanks in the diagram, filling in the picture John was communicating. Each line in the diagram will have one term from the word bank.

Lesson 2.1

WORD BANK:

Red Sea

New Nation

Leave Slavery

Baptism

Repent

Egypt

Israel

EVALUATION

1. In the eyes of the world, what were John's qualifications for the job God gave him? _____
_____
_____

2. What qualifications did God give John? Did He give John special education or a special title? _____
_____
_____
_____

3. What message did John preach? _____
_____
_____

4. What picture did John's baptizing ministry present? _____
_____
_____

57

LESSON 2.2

Jesus' Baptism

UNIT 2

NOTES TO THE TEACHER

Lesson Theme - Jesus' credentials validated through baptism

Jesus' baptism was God's explanation of Jesus' identity and purpose in Israel. His baptism was a significant event and its symbolic import was multifaceted. Therefore, this lesson can't be easily reduced to a single central idea. Clearly, Jesus took part in John's baptism because He wanted to identify with the *new people* that John was calling out of Israel. But Jesus was not *just* a member of this new people; He was the head. He was a new Joshua; leading the new people on conquest in the land. Looking at it from another angle, Jesus' baptism fulfilled the history of Israel and showed that He *is* the new Israel. Finally, Jesus' baptism identified Him as high priest from a new priestly order. To sum it up, Jesus' baptism declared the following regarding Jesus:

1. He was identified with the *new people* John was calling out of Israel (see Lesson 2.1).
2. He was the new Joshua; the head of the *new people* (see OT Lesson 6.2).
3. He was the new Israel (see OT Lesson 5.4).
4. He was a new high priest from a new priesthood.

John the Baptist came to prepare Israel for the Messiah (Lesson 2.1). He did this by calling the nation to the wilderness to repent and be baptized, and therefore created a new people out of the old Israel. Those who were baptized were constituted as a new nation much like the first generation of Israel was constituted as a nation

OVERVIEW

Jesus had returned from His exodus to Egypt, anticipated His ministry in the temple and grown up in His earthly father's house. Next, He met His forerunner John in the wilderness. Jesus underwent John's baptism, identifying with the new people John was calling out of Israel. Furthermore, Jesus' baptism continues the picture that Jesus is the new Israel and identifies Him as the new Joshua. God affirmed Jesus in His ministry by sending the Holy Spirit upon Him and speaking from heaven.

SOURCE MATERIAL

- **Matthew 3:13-16**
- Mark 1:9-11
- Luke 2:21-22
- John 1:29-34

after crossing (and being baptized in) the Red Sea (OT Lesson 5.4). Jesus "fulfilled all righteousness" (Matt 3:15) when He partook in John's baptism and became a member of this new people. But He was not just a member of the new people; He was their leader. He was the new Joshua who led the new Israel in conquest of the land, defeating the enemies of Israel: demons, disease and death.

Beyond this, Jesus Himself is the new Israel who had returned from Egypt, was baptized in the Jordan and was tempted in the wilderness for 40 days, just like Israel was tested in the wilderness for 40 years; He succeeded where Israel failed.

Unit 2: Jesus' Ministry Begins

OBJECTIVES

Feel...

- security in the fatherhood of God, since He accepted His beloved Son before He had done anything.
- peace with God, since He accepts us freely in Jesus Christ.

Understand...

- the multifaceted symbolic import of Jesus' baptism.
    - It identified Him with the "new people."
    - He is the new Joshua: the head of the "new people."
    - He is the new Israel.
    - He was consecrated as a high priest in His baptism.
- that God spoke favor to Jesus before His ministry even began.

Apply this understanding by...

- believing that you are accepted in Christ apart from works.
- analyzing your life to see if you are living as though you are accepted in Christ.
- repenting if necessary and resting in the grace of God.

Jesus' baptism was also priestly ordination. Like the original nation of Israel, the new Israel was called to be a nation of priests. Jesus was baptized as the new high priest of this new priestly order. Under the Old Covenant, the Aaronic priests were baptized (washed) with water to be cleansed and therefore qualified as priests. Priests bore the sins of the people and offered sacrifices on their behalf. Jesus "fulfilled all righteousness" by symbolically taking on the sins of the new nation and being symbolically washed of those sins.

God validated the symbolic import of Jesus' baptism by speaking from heaven and sending the Holy Spirit upon Him. Jesus operated His entire ministry out of His confident standing in God's favor. He did not work in order to find peace with God; He worked *because* He already had it.

This concept provides the foundation for us as Christians in understanding our own baptism. Take some time to really reflect on the significance of Jesus' baptism; we will draw on it when we get to Acts. Like Jesus, when we are baptized as Christians, we are identifying with the new people: the Church. In our baptism, God tells us that we are accepted in Christ.

APPLICATION

The application for this lesson is a "believe this..." rather than a "do this..." application. Whether you have been baptized or not, if you have believed in Christ, you have been accepted by God *in Christ*. Your baptism is a physical reminder of the fact that you are one with Christ in baptism, and therefore God accepts you based on the fact that God accepted Christ.

ADDITIONAL NOTES

Baptism is a picture of death and resurrection. Therefore, by being baptized, Jesus symbolically died and rose again to become a part of the new Israel. His baptism foreshadows His later death and resurrection through which the Church would be created.

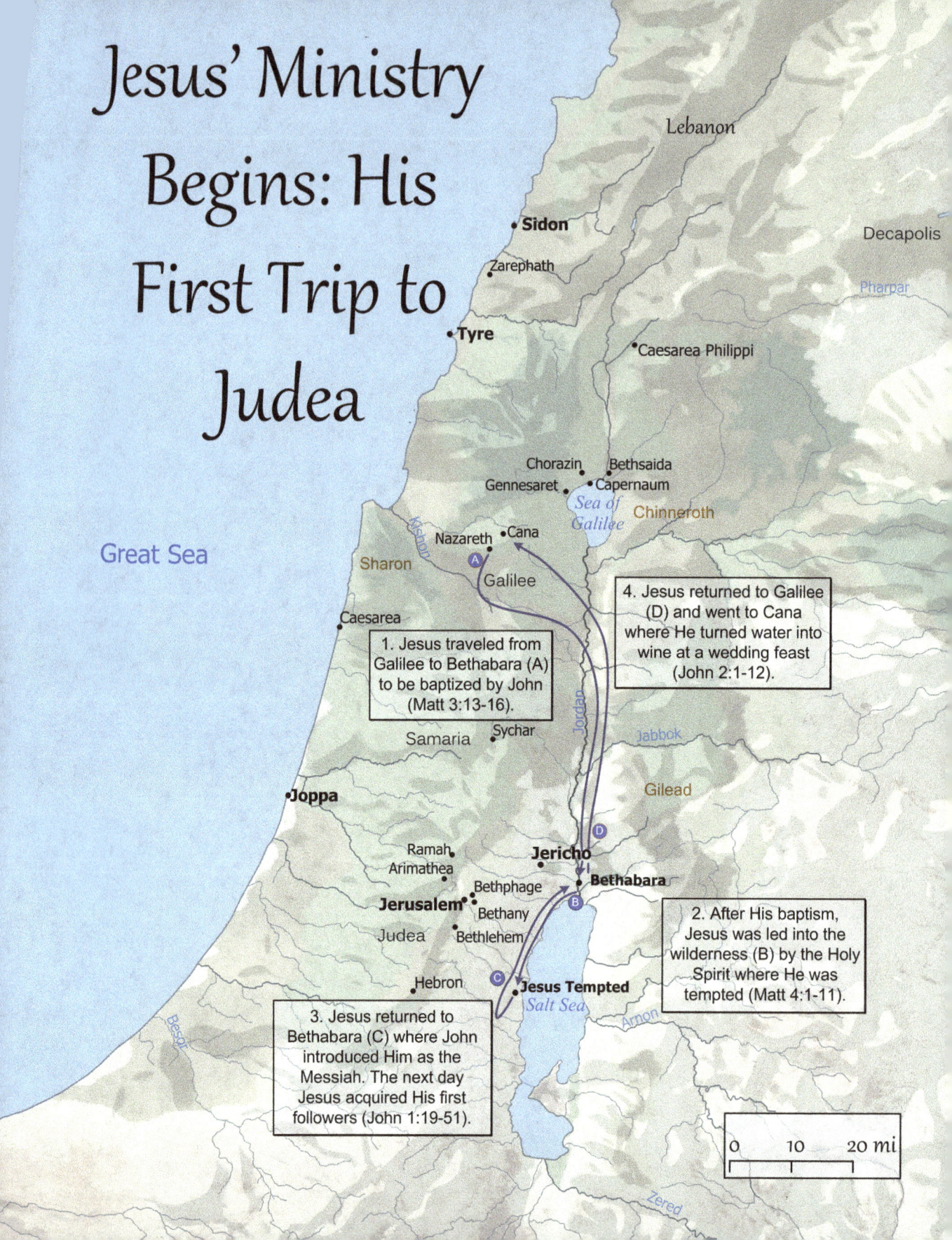

Lesson 2.2

ACTIVITIES

1. The Meaning of Water. Water is a part of our lives every day. But water is both a blessing and a source of hardship. The meaning of water in the Bible is built on the meaning of water in everyday life. Fill in the two lists below then answer the questions that follow.

Good things water does	Bad things water does

In general, is water a good thing, a bad thing, or both? _____
_____
_____
_____

What does the fact that something so necessary to life can also be the source of death teach you about God's world? _____
_____
_____
_____

Unit 2: Jesus' Ministry Begins

Why do you think God chose baptism as the symbol of what it means to be a Christian in light of what you now know about water? _____

_____

_____

_____

_____

2. Journal Time. Consider whether you are living as though you have already been accepted by God or if you are trying to work hard to earn God's acceptance. Answer the following questions in the space below.

How do you picture God thinking about you—as a critical judge, inspecting your every move, waiting to point out and punish any wrong that you do, or as a loving Father, knowing all about you because He created you and loves you? _____

_____

_____

_____

_____

When you do something "good," do you think that maybe you have earned God's acceptance or moved up a little higher on His "nice list"? Likewise, if you sin, do you feel that God no longer accepts you or that you are now on His "naughty list"? _____

_____

_____

_____

_____

Think about your relationship with your earthly parents and how your relationship with your dad and mom (as you were growing up, or presently if relevant) affects your view of God. _____

_____

_____

_____

Lesson 2.2

EVALUATION

1. What does Jesus' baptism tell us? _____
_____
_____
_____

2. What does God's response to His baptism tell us about Jesus? _____
_____
_____
_____

LESSON 2.3

Jesus' Fasting and Temptation

UNIT 2

NOTES TO THE TEACHER

Lesson Theme - Defeating powerful temptation is the springboard into powerful ministry.
Jesus succeeded where Adam and Eve failed—He conquered the basic temptations that the whole human race continually faces. Jesus succeeded where the exodus generation failed—He spent 40 days being tested in the wilderness and passed the test. After passing the test, He was released to "conquer the land" by preaching and working miracles.

The passages don't emphasize this next point, but pay particular attention to Luke 4:2. We are told about three particular temptations at the end of the 40-day period, but the devil tempted Jesus *the whole time.* For 40 days, the devil went after Jesus with everything he had—imagine it! At the end of the 40 days, the devil had three big temptations left, and these three are the ones Matthew and Luke tell us about in detail. (Note that Matthew and Luke recount the three temptations in a different order. This lesson will follow Luke's order.)

In order to get Jesus' temptations in perspective, recall Adam and Eve's temptations. Adam was not deceived; he fell into the temptation of directly challenging God's command. Eve was deceived, and take a good look at the key points of her deception: "when the woman saw that the tree was good for food, that it was pleasant to the eyes, and a tree desirable to make one wise, she took of its fruit and ate" (Gen 3:6). In Eve's perception:

OVERVIEW

Immediately after His baptism, the Spirit took Jesus into the wilderness, where He fasted and was tempted as Adam and Eve were once tempted. Unlike them, He passed the test with flying colors.

SOURCE MATERIAL

- **Luke 4:1-13**
- Matthew 4:1-11
- Mark 1:12-23
- Genesis 3:1-7
- 1 John 2:15-17

- The fruit was good for food, that is, lust of the flesh, an appeal to the bodily appetites.
- The fruit was pleasant to the eyes, that is, lust of the eyes, an appeal to sight.
- The fruit was desirable to make one wise, that is, the pride of life, an appeal to the desire to achieve personal greatness.

Jesus was tempted at exactly these same points. He knew perfectly well that doing anything the devil wanted Him to do was going to be against the will of the Father, which was Adam's temptation. But the devil also hit Him at the key points that were so persuasive to Eve.

Eve saw that the fruit was good for food. Jesus hadn't eaten in 40 days, and He was hungry

Unit 2: Jesus' Ministry Begins

OBJECTIVES

Feel...

- admiration for Jesus' standing up to 40 days of continual temptation by Satan himself.
- hope that temptation can be defeated through Christ.
- hope that pushing through temptation brings fruitfulness and power on the other side.

Understand...

- that after Jesus had been singled out as God's beloved Son, it was necessary for Him to be tested.
- that Jesus was tested in the same ways Adam and Eve were tested.
- that these temptations were *real* temptations, appealing to Jesus' real desires.
- that these are the very same temptations that we face every single day.

Apply this understanding by...

- identifying a particular temptation that's a problem for you.
- formulating a plan for dealing with this temptation similar to how Jesus dealt with His temptations.
- dreaming with God about what "conquering the land" might look like in your own life after you have successfully mastered the temptation.

(Luke 4:2). The Spirit took Him out into the desert, and Jesus' job was to trust the Spirit to provide for Him. The devil tempted Jesus as he once tempted Eve, to forget about God's provision and take care of Himself (Luke 4:3). While Eve took the fruit, Jesus resisted the temptation to turn the stones into bread.

Eve saw that the fruit was pleasant to the eyes. Satan took Jesus to a high mountain and showed Him all the kingdoms of the world and all their glory (Luke 4:5). Jesus saw it all, and Satan offered it all to Him. It's important to realize that Jesus didn't refuse him because He didn't want the kingdoms of the world. He did want them, and He does want them. But what Satan offered Jesus was a way to have them without going to the cross. "Just fall down and worship," Satan said, "and I'll just give you the whole thing without a fight." While Eve ate the fruit, Jesus rejected the offer.

Eve saw that the fruit was desirable to make her wise. God put her on the earth to be His image, to rule over it as He would. The fruit would make her like God, knowing good and evil, and therefore better able to do what God had called her to do. And so she took it—aiming for God's goal, but failing to get there God's way. The devil took Jesus to the highest point of the temple, the top corner of Solomon's Porch above the Kidron Valley (Luke 4:9). From there it was at least 450 feet to the ground (equivalent to a 45-story building). It was on this high point that the priest would stand to see the dawn and signal the beginning of the morning sacrifice. Some of the rabbis taught that the Messiah would fulfill Malachi 3:1 by coming to this very spot. "Fling yourself off here," the devil said, "in front of everybody. Let them all see the angels appear to catch you so you won't fall. What a way to announce yourself to the nation!" Again, remember that Jesus *did* want the nation to know who He was, and He *did* want to do miracles, so that they would believe. This was something the Father had called Him to do. But the Father had called Him to do it in a different way. The devil was offering Jesus a way that seemed to make a lot of sense—but it was not the Father's way. Jesus trusted the Father to bring it about His way, and turned the devil down.

The *way* Jesus turned down each of the temptations is also worth exploring a little. In each case, He quoted Deuteronomy, but beyond that, His strategy was slightly different each time.

Entrust your needs to God. Jesus responded to the temptation to turn stones to bread with Deuteronomy 8:3, which recalls Israel's time in the wilderness: "So He humbled you, allowed you to hunger, and fed you with manna which you did not know nor did your fathers know, that He might make you know that man shall not live by bread alone; but man lives by every word that proceeds from the mouth of the LORD." When Israel was in exactly the same situation (stuck in the desert with no food), they complained. Jesus learned the lesson that Israel did not, and He did what they should have done—relied on God for food.

Don't get distracted by what you see. Jesus rejected the temptation to take all the kingdoms of the earth in exchange for worshipping the devil with Deuteronomy 6:13. Look at it in context: "So it shall be, when the LORD your God brings you into the land of which He swore to your fathers, to Abraham, Isaac, and Jacob, to give you large and beautiful cities which you did not build, houses full of all good things, which you did not fill, hewn-out wells which you did not dig, vineyards and olive trees which you did not plant—when you have eaten and are full—then beware, lest you forget the LORD who brought you out of the land of Egypt, from the house of bondage. *You shall fear the LORD your God and serve Him,* and shall take oaths in His name. You shall not go after other gods, the gods of the peoples who are all around you..." (Deut 6:10-13, emphasis added). God wanted to give His people all these things. The warning is that when they have all these blessings surrounding them, they should not get so distracted by it all that they forget to worship Yahweh and begin to worship other gods. The devil was showing Jesus a vision of success—to simply be given the world He came to save—but the price was exactly what God warned Israel not to do when they had achieved success. Jesus saw the parallel—don't let what you see tempt you away from God—and quoted the relevant passage of Scripture.

Trust that God's path to the goal is best. In response to the temptation to announce His ministry by throwing Himself off the pinnacle of the temple and be publicly rescued by angels, Jesus remembered Deuteronomy 6:16 (the very next verse after the passage above): "You shall not tempt the LORD your God as you tempted Him in Massah." In order for the command to make sense, we need to look back at the situation, which is recorded in Exodus 17:1-7. Israel complained against the Lord, but the particular thing to notice is the last line of verse 7: "they tempted the LORD, saying, 'Is the LORD among us or not?'" Israel knew that God had led them into the desert, but they doubted His way of doing things, and questioned whether He was really going to be there for them when they needed Him most. What they needed to do (and failed to do) was simply trust that God's way of handling the situation was best. The command not to tempt the Lord as Israel once did in Massah is a command to trust that God's way is best. Jesus did trust and quoted this command to resist the devil.

Unit 2: Jesus' Ministry Begins

Notice also that all three of these passages that Jesus quoted are from Deuteronomy. This was not an accident. Jesus was being tested in the wilderness like Israel was tested in the wilderness, and if He passed the test, then He could go and conquer the land.

Deuteronomy is a long speech given to the conquest generation to teach them God's Law, to warn them against the failures of their parents, the exodus generation, and to prepare them to conquer the land. If you want to conquer the land, then Deuteronomy is the book you need to pay attention to—as Paul also says in 1 Corinthians 10:1-11.

It's important to grasp what was happening here in terms of the whole sweep of the biblical Story. Adam and Eve failed when the devil tempted them along exactly these lines; the exodus generation was also tested in the wilderness and failed, but Jesus succeeded. He took everything the devil could throw at Him for 40 days, and He prevailed. Now that He passed the test, like the conquest generation, He was released to go and conquer the land.

It's also important to understand three key things about the aftermath of the test.

First, angels came and ministered to Jesus (Matt 4:11, Mark 1:13). God does take care of His own. He allows us to be tested, but He sees to it that we are also taken care of.

Second, the devil departed from Jesus "until an opportune time" (Luke 4:13). Until the last judgment, the devil has been given the authority to "[walk] about like a roaring lion, seeking whom he may devour" (1 Pet 5:8). He flees temporarily, but he does come back, even for Jesus. When we win a spiritual victory, we need to remember that the devil will be back for another round.

Third, Jesus was released to begin His ministry. Luke records that He "returned in the power of the Spirit to Galilee, and news of Him went out through all the surrounding region" (Luke 4:14). Testing is the prelude to power. If we want to see God break out in our lives and do amazing things, then we *must* persevere through temptation. The flip side of this is that we should be encouraged when the testing is severe, because it wouldn't be that bad unless there was something really big on the other side.

APPLICATION

We ought to handle temptations similarly to how Jesus did: trust God with our needs, not get distracted by what we see, and trust that God's way to the goal is the best way. We should also understand that God will see that we're taken care of when it's over, that the devil will come back for another round later, and that testing is the launchpad for powerful ministry.

ACTIVITIES

1. Understanding the Nature of Temptation. Read Genesis 3:1-7, Matthew 4:1-11, and 1 John 2:15-17. Use the table below to compare and contrast the temptations in these passages.

Genesis 3:1-17	Matthew 4:1-11	1 John 2:15-17

2. Journal Time: Dealing with Temptation. In your journal or the space below answer the following questions regarding temptation.

What is a temptation in your own life that seems to beat you regularly? _____
_____
_____
_____

What were Jesus' three temptations? _____
_____
_____
_____

Unit 2: Jesus' Ministry Begins

Which of Jesus' three temptations is your temptation like? _____
_____
_____
_____
_____

What might it look like to resist your temptation in a way Jesus would? _____
_____
_____
_____
_____

Jesus' 40 days in the desert being tempted by the devil were the launchpad for three years of incredible ministry, all culminating in the crucifixion, resurrection, and ascension. What new things might open up for you, once you have beaten your temptation? Spend some time praying and thinking about this before you answer. _____
_____
_____
_____
_____
_____
_____
_____

Lesson 2.3

EVALUATION

1. What were Jesus' three temptations? _____
_____
_____
_____
_____

2. Why would these three things have been wrong? _____
_____
_____
_____
_____
_____
_____
_____
_____

3. How did Jesus resist each of the temptations? _____
_____
_____
_____
_____
_____
_____
_____
_____
_____
_____

LESSON 2.4

John Passed the Baton to Jesus

UNIT 2

NOTES TO THE TEACHER

Lesson Theme - John fulfilled his calling to be a forerunner, becoming less while Jesus became greater.

Jesus began His ministry in the summer or fall of A.D. 29. Before this, He was essentially unknown in Israel. John, on the other hand, had already created quite a stir. He was not a *minor* prophet preaching to the faithful few in the wilderness; crowds were flocking to the desert to be baptized by him. Mark says that "Then all the land of Judea, and those from Jerusalem, went out to him" (Mark 1:5). His was a ministry to the common Israelite, but eventually he drew the interest of the Pharisees and Sadducees who came out to question him. In short, John was a *big* deal. But his calling was never to be the headliner; he was just the opening act. When it came time for Jesus to begin His ministry, John humbly pointed to the Messiah and receded into the background.

John's ministry began before Jesus' did, and there was a period of overlap where they were both operating effective ministries in Israel. Several important things happened during this overlap period. First, John was continually pointing to Jesus, such that Jesus' ministry grew while John's shrunk; this was John's purpose all along. Second, several of John's disciples left John to follow Jesus. Finally, John spoke boldly against Herod and the wicked things he had done which led to his imprisonment.

John began his ministry shortly before Jesus did; at the most, perhaps a year before. Even

OVERVIEW

John's ministry began before Jesus' did, and a great number of people came to repent and be baptized by him. But he was always looking forward to Jesus. When Jesus arrived, John humbly submitted to God's calling and became less as Christ became greater. Ultimately, John was imprisoned for his boldness and died at the hands of Herod; but he will always be remembered for making much of Jesus.

SOURCE MATERIAL

- **John 1:35-51, John 3:22-36**
- **Matthew 11:1-4**, 5-19
- **Mark** 1:4-8, 14-15, **6:14-29**
- **Luke** 3:15-18, **19-20**

before Jesus came on the scene, John's message consistently pointed forward to Him (Luke 3:16). During that time, John's call to repentance in the wilderness generated a great following.

In the summer of A.D. 29, Jesus was baptized by John and then taken to the wilderness where He was tempted, while John continued to preach the gospel. When Jesus returned from the wilderness, John announced the coming of the Messiah, and Jesus' public ministry began (John 1:19-42).

When Jesus returned from the wilderness, He was still an unknown figure. He stood in the crowd while John preached and went unnoticed by everyone except John who said, "I baptize

75

Unit 2: Jesus' Ministry Begins

OBJECTIVES

Feel...

- impressed with John's humility and faithfulness to his calling.
- sad that John had doubts later on, but thankful that John is still remembered for his faithfulness.

Understand...

- what John did to point to Jesus both before and after Jesus' baptism.
    - John announced that the Messiah was coming before He came.
    - John announced Jesus when He was in the crowds afterward.
    - John pointed his disciples to Jesus.
- roughly how John's and Jesus' ministries overlapped.
- what caused John's imprisonment.
- how John died.

Apply this understanding by...

- laying aside self-seeking and making much of Jesus.
- beginning to understand your calling.

with water, but there stands One among you whom you do not know. It is He who, coming after me, is preferred before me, whose sandal strap I am not worthy to loose" (John 1:26-27). The following day, John went a step further and boldly directed attention to Jesus and announced the coming of the "Lamb of God" (John 1:29).

On the following day, John directed two of his disciples toward Jesus. As Jesus was walking by, John told his disciples, "Look, the Lamb of God!" (John 1:29). In other words, "What are you doing standing around with me? The *Lamb of God* is on the move!" Immediately those two left John and followed Jesus. The apostle John was probably one of the two and the other was Andrew. Andrew immediately went and got his brother Simon Peter who followed Jesus as well. The following day, Jesus gained two more disciples when He issued a call to Philip and Nathanael.

Both Jesus and John were then actively engaged in preaching the gospel at the same time. John continued in Judea while Jesus went back to Galilee for the wedding at Cana then on to Capernaum and finally back to Jerusalem for the Passover. It was at this Passover that Jesus' ministry kicked into high gear; He cleared the temple courts and began preaching and baptizing in the Judean countryside.

John was also baptizing in the same region at this time, but fewer people were attracted to him and more were going to Jesus. During this period, John turned his rhetoric toward Herod and landed himself in prison (where he would spend the rest of his life). Meanwhile, Jesus had gained a substantial amount of notoriety and decided to continue His ministry in Galilee and put some distance between Himself and the hostile Judean leadership (Mark 1:14-15, John 4:1-3).

Matthew later records a somewhat surprising interaction between Jesus and John. While Jesus was preaching in Galilee, John sent some of his disciples to Him asking if He really was the Messiah, or if He was just a *second* forerunner with the real Messiah yet to come (Matt 11:3). It is unclear what brought about John's doubt; perhaps he expected the Messiah to spend more time in Jerusalem and set up His kingdom. Whatever it was, Jesus sent back a message assuring him that He was doing all the things the

Messiah was expected to do. Early on, John was so convinced that Jesus was the Messiah that he pointed to Him and said "Look, the Lamb of God!" but later he doubted. Jesus reassured him and then said to the crowds that "among those born of women there has not risen one greater than John the Baptist" (Matt 11:11). The point is that if someone as faithful as John went through a low spot, then we shouldn't be surprised when we or those we look up to also struggle with our faith.

John's rhetoric against Herod led to his imprisonment and, ultimately, to his death. Herod had promised to give his wife's daughter whatever she wanted. She (at the urging of Herodias, Herod's wife) asked for John's head on a platter. Herod, not wanting to lose face, granted her request (Mark 6:14-29).

So John's life ended with an episode of doubt and a premature death, but he will always be remembered for his faithfulness and boldness.

APPLICATION

John consistently and faithfully pointed toward Jesus as he was called to do. He was never intended to be the headliner; he was simply a forerunner. John knew that the most important thing was faithfulness to God's calling on his life. If you or I had John's calling, we might have kept the audience for ourselves so that we could have a legacy of our own.

Like John, we are called to make much of Jesus. We must become less, and He must become more. If we are honest with ourselves, the desire to be one of the "cool kids" never goes away. And along with that desire comes the temptation to speak honestly about our convictions. Or, conversely, we want to draw attention to ourselves with our words instead of pointing others to Jesus.

To take it in a different direction, some people are called to be the front person and some people are called to support them. Think of Paul and Barnabas. Those of you who are called to be out front will need a greater helping of humility; those that work as support for others should be content if that is their calling.

The broader issue here is the question of calling. God has given everyone a certain set of gifts and certain tasks to accomplish with those gifts. You aren't going to discern all the details of your calling today, but if you haven't started seeking God's specific call on your life, there's no time like the present. What direction do the strengths and gifts point you in terms of you calling? What have others observed about your particular gifting and calling?

Unit 2: Jesus' Ministry Begins

ACTIVITIES

1. Timeline. Using John 1-3 and Mark 1:1-14 construct a rough timeline of the events of John and Jesus' ministries on the line below. Actual times between events are often unknown, but include them where they are given. Make sure to include all the following events, but you can include more if you want.

The following events should be included on your timeline (given in no particular order):

- Jesus' ministry began.
- John began preaching in the wilderness.
- John was beheaded.
- Jesus went to Galilee for the wedding at Cana.
- John was imprisoned.
- John pointed to announce the Lamb of God.
- John baptized Jesus.
- Jesus went to Galilee.
- John pointed his disciples toward Jesus.

_____

2. Journal Time: Your Calling. John the Baptist was created by God to be this wild wilderness man who was to make a big deal of Jesus and then fade into the background. He was most fulfilled as a person when he followed this calling. Write in the space below, answering the following questions. What is something you feel most fulfilled doing?_____

_____
_____
_____
_____
_____

Lesson 2.4

How can you do this thing to glorify God? _____
_____
_____
_____
_____
_____
_____
_____
_____
_____
_____

EVALUATION

1. Whose ministry started first, Jesus' or John's? _____

2. Name three things John did to draw attention away from himself and toward Jesus. _____
_____
_____
_____
_____

3. Describe what happened during the period of overlap between Jesus' and John's ministries. _____
_____
_____

4. What did John do that landed him in prison? _____
_____

5. How did John die? _____
_____
_____

LESSON 2.5

Water into Wine

NOTES TO THE TEACHER

Lesson Theme - Jesus began the new creation. In this lesson, we learn how Jesus symbolically revealed what the new creation was all about; the Old Covenant's rituals of washing were transformed into the New Covenant's emphasis on feasting. The Old Covenant wasn't a dead covenant; it was oriented around water, and water is life. But the New Covenant is more glorious than the Old Covenant since it is a covenant of wine. Wine is glorified water, liquid rest. The Old Covenant was built around religious ceremonies and rituals. The New Covenant was inaugurated with a wedding feast.

The gospel of John is the Genesis of the new creation. It starts the same way Genesis 1 does. Then, just like the first creation account, it gives a sequence of seven days. The first seven days of Jesus' ministry (reckoning the beginning of His ministry from *after* He was baptized and tested in the wilderness, commencing when John announced His coming in John 1:19-28) are presented as the first seven days of the new creation. On the first day, Jesus was veiled, but He was there, and John announced His coming (John 1:19-28). On the second day ("the next day"—John 1:29) John introduced Jesus as the Messiah (John 1:29-34). On the third day, several of John's disciples followed Jesus; and on the fourth, Jesus called two additional disciples: Philip and Nathanael. John 2 begins with another chronological marker, "On the third day there was a wedding in Cana of Galilee" (John 2:1). Each of the previous days in this sequence are noted as taking place immediately after the previous day ("on the next day"). However, the wedding took place on the third day after Jesus called Philip and Nathanael, making it the seventh day of Jesus' ministry: the seventh day of the new creation.

OVERVIEW

Jesus' ministry was the beginning of the new creation, and on the seventh day He revealed His glory at a wedding feast by turning ceremonial water into wine. By this miracle, Jesus demonstrated that the New Covenant was a covenant of celebration. As a result, His disciples believed in Him.

SOURCE MATERIAL

John 2:1-11

In Lesson 2.2 we learned that water is liquid life. Wine is liquid rest: transformed and glorified life. As we have paid careful attention to John's time markers, we have seen that this miracle took place on the seventh day; the Sabbath of the new creation. The new creation is a creation characterized by wine instead of by water. By turning water into wine, Jesus was announcing the new creation *within* the old. Jesus brought about a new creation by transforming the old.

Many of Jesus' miracles dealt directly with human suffering; He healed diseases, cast out demons, calmed the storm. In short, He conquered the fall. Contrast these with the miracle at Cana, and it looks like a simple magic trick. Few were

Unit 2: Jesus' Ministry Begins

OBJECTIVES

Feel...

- awe that Jesus was a winemaker.
- excitement that the New Covenant is about celebration.

Understand...

- the differences between the water of the Old Covenant and the water and wine of the New Covenant.
- that the first seven days of Jesus' ministry were the first seven days of the new creation.
- that Jesus turned water into wine on the seventh day of the new creation.
- that water is life and wine is rest.
- the significance of turning *ceremonial* water into wine.
- the significance of this miracle being performed at a wedding.
- why Jesus performed this miracle even though His "hour [had] not yet come."
- that Jesus involved the servants in the miracle, but didn't tell them why they were to fill the pots with water.

Apply this understanding by...

- evaluating your life to see if you do as Mary directed the servants: "Whatever He says to you, do it."

there to witness the occasion, and the miracle seems of little consequence; Jesus might as well have pulled a rabbit out of a hat.

But this miracle was so much more than that. It was a symbolic announcement and foreshadowing of the nature of the new creation. It was a clear message to His disciples that He was the Messiah of a new age. Jesus communicated these things in two ways: first, by turning water for ceremonial cleansing into celebratory wine and second, by doing it at a wedding feast.

There was nothing wrong with the Old Covenant. In fact it was life-giving to the Israelites who would receive God's promises. Remember the first generation that came out of Egypt? After they crossed the Red Sea, God gave them water *from a rock.* This wasn't just a bit of kind magic in the wilderness to quench their thirst. It was a symbolic announcement; God gives the water of life to those who simply trust Him. The gods of the Egyptians were a dry well, and the children of Israel had just gotten a mouthful of sand from the bottom. The Old Covenant had loads of water; water for ordaining the priests, water for washing their hands, and water lined up outside of Solomon's temple. But it was prophetic water, not the real thing; it wasn't *living* water.

John 2:6 tells us that Jesus used the stone water jars that were for ceremonial washing to hold the water He was going to turn into wine. The Old Covenant required a variety of washings, but the Pharisees had multiplied these requirements. A wedding hosted according to the customs of the day (not just the Old Testament Law) might have required numerous washings, which was no doubt the reason there were so many water jars at this wedding celebration (six pots each capable of holding 20-30 gallons). Consider how a good Pharisee might have responded when he went to perform a ritual washing after Jesus had filled those pots with wine; he would have been shocked and appalled at Jesus' lack of reverence. Jesus was sending a message: the New Covenant replaces human rituals with a party overflowing with good wine.

Jesus launched His public ministry at a wedding, not with a somber ritual at the temple. Jesus was not just signaling the celebratory nature of the New Covenant. He was announcing that heaven and earth were being reunited. The bridegroom had arrived and He was looking for a bride. The New Covenant is about God and man becoming one *in Christ*.

However, it was not yet time for the *real* wedding feast. The bride had not yet been formed and clothed in her wedding garments; the Church was still to come. Notice Jesus' brief interaction with his mother. Mary, knowing Jesus' calling, directed her attention to her son when the supplies ran dry: "They have no wine" (John 2:3). Jesus understood what she was implying, but demurred, "Woman, what does your concern have to do with Me? My hour has not yet come" (John 2:4). Jesus performed the miracle anyway, but prefaced it by indicating that His actions were ahead of their time; the ultimate wedding banquet was yet to come.

This miracle was for the disciples, to establish that Jesus was indeed the Messiah and confirm their faith in Him. No one at the wedding celebration knew about this miracle apart from Mary, the servants and Jesus' six disciples (that's all He had at this point). This miracle was the first of the signs Jesus performed (there are seven signs in John that lead up to the final sign: Jesus' resurrection), and He did it to reveal His glory to His disciples. As a result, John tells us that they "believed in Him" (John 2:11).

APPLICATION

Many of Jesus' miracles involved others in some way; in this one, Jesus enlisted the help of the servants of the house and had them fill the stone water pots. Jesus invited others into His work. Notice what Mary told them: "Whatever He says to you, do it" (John 2:5). They followed His orders to the word and took part in the revelation of His glory (John 2:11).

As priests, we are called to obey the simple commands of Jesus. We, like these servants, may not be told *why*, but we can be sure that if we are following the commands of Jesus, we are being called into something great. In general terms, we can know this: when we obey Jesus' commands, we reveal the character of Jesus to the world; we reveal His glory.

ACTIVITIES

1. Think it Through. Think back to the last party you went to. Were there enough drinks for everyone to have some? Any leftover at the end? _____

_____

Why is it important to have more than enough drinks at party?_____

_____

Unit 2: Jesus' Ministry Begins

Why does God want us to celebrate under the New Covenant? _____
_____
_____
_____
_____

2. The Servants' Perspective. Imagine that you were one of the servants at the wedding and that Jesus instructed you to help with His miracle.

Would you feel excited to be a part of it? _____
_____
_____
_____

Would you think that the directions Jesus gave you were strange or perhaps unnecessary? _____
_____
_____
_____
_____

How would you feel once seeing the result of Jesus' miracle? _____
_____
_____
_____
_____
_____
_____
_____

Lesson 2.5

EVALUATION

1. In what way did the water of the Old Covenant differ from the water of the New Covenant? _____
_____
_____

2. John presents the beginning of Jesus' ministry as the first seven days of the new creation. On what day did the water to wine miracle take place? _____

3. What is the significance of the seventh day, and why was it appropriate for this particular miracle?
_____
_____
_____

4. What are the symbolic meanings for water and wine? _____
_____
_____

5. What was the purpose of the pots that Jesus used for turning water into wine? _____
_____
_____

6. What message did Jesus send by turning ceremonial water into wine? _____
_____
_____
_____

7. What is the significance of Jesus performing this miracle at a wedding? _____
_____
_____

8. Before Jesus performed this miracle, He told Mary that His "hour had not yet come." Why did He do the miracle anyway? _____
_____

LESSON 2.6

From Darkness to Light: Jesus and Nicodemus

UNIT 2

NOTES TO THE TEACHER

Lesson Theme - The need for the new birth
As we have seen in previous lessons, Jesus was beginning a new creation within the old and that meant that everything needed to be made new. We are made new by the new birth which comes by means of faith in Jesus Christ.

In many ways, the events of this lesson are the practical beginning of Jesus' public ministry. Jesus had given hints at His mission (water to wine—transforming the old into the new creation), but in this lesson He gets serious about it. He walked in the temple to find that the court had been turned into a shopping mall where the wealthy were extorting the poor worshipers. The temple, Jesus' Father's house, was full of death, and so He ran them out (John 2:15).

When the Judeans asked Him where He got His authority, Jesus told them, "Destroy this temple, and in three days I will raise it up" (John 2:19). They didn't get it, of course; they didn't understand the need for a new creation. In the new creation, Jesus' body was the new temple where men would find the living God. Many heard His message and saw His miracles and believed in Him, but He wouldn't entrust Himself to them (John 2:23-25). They were attracted to Him and believed in Him, but they didn't understand His real purpose. Therefore they couldn't be trusted to take part in His mission.

The Nicodemus story is a specific example of the general phenomenon discussed in John 2:23-25. Nicodemus believed that Jesus was from God

OVERVIEW

Jesus traveled to Jerusalem for the Passover feast and really kicked His ministry into high gear. He created a stir in the temple by running out the money changers and began preaching and performing miracles. Many believed in Him, but Jesus would not entrust Himself to them. One of the untrustworthy folks who believed in Jesus because of the signs, Nicodemus, came to Jesus at night to inquire further into His message and mission. Jesus began by explaining the necessity of the new birth, which set up His explanation of His unique qualifications and mission to save the world and invite people into fellowship with God.

SOURCE MATERIAL

- John 2:13-3:21
- Numbers 21
- Psalms 16-17
- Proverbs 12:15-16

based on the signs, but he didn't really understand what Jesus was about; he came to Jesus at night, away from prying eyes. He couldn't yet be trusted with God's mission in the world.

The singular and plural use of "you" is very important in this discussion. These are distinct words in Greek (*su* and *humeis* respectively). In order to help you track this in your English Bible, a translation that makes it plain is appended to this lesson. Pay particular attention to John 3:7,

Unit 2: Jesus' Ministry Begins

OBJECTIVES

Feel...

- Nicodemus' perplexity at the way Jesus was speaking to him.
- gratitude for the salvation that God has provided in Christ.
- gratitude for the invitation into life with God, now.

Understand...

- why Jesus ran the animal hawkers and money changers out of the temple.
- why Jesus wouldn't entrust Himself to those who believed in Him.
- the need for the new birth.
- the connection between the bronze serpent story and the Jesus story.
- Jesus' unique qualification to teach heavenly truth.
- Jesus' unique mission in providing salvation for the world.
- Jesus' invitation to come into the light and walk with God now, in this life.

Apply this understanding by...

- employing Psalm 16 to celebrate our salvation.
- considering how you might better accept Jesus' invitation to come into the light.

11-12, where the plural "you" is a reference to the nation of Israel at large, not Nicodemus in particular.

Remember that Nicodemus believed Jesus was from God in a general way, but didn't understand Jesus' mission or message. Jesus began to answer Nicodemus' unspoken questions by challenging him with the need for every person to be born again (John 3:3).

There are several different views on what it means to be "born of water." Based on the parallels between John 3:5 and 6, we take the position that it's a reference to physical birth. (Another common view takes it as a reference to baptism, but in symbolic terms, baptism is death and resurrection, not birth.)

The Greek word translated "again" (John 3:3, 7) can also mean "from above." Nicodemus clearly understood it as "again" in his initial response, but Jesus was using the play on words and meant it to be understood from both angles.

From John 3:7 and 10, it would seem that Jesus thought Nicodemus should already know about the need for a second birth. In John 3:5-7, Jesus made the argument: He was seeking to lead Nicodemus to the conclusion that the kingdom is spiritual, and so a spiritual birth is required to enter it. This opened the door for Jesus to talk about His unique role in bringing people into the kingdom of God.

In John 3:10-13, Jesus made the case that He was uniquely qualified to teach heavenly things, because He came from heaven.

In John 3:14-15, Jesus introduced His own role in leading people into the kingdom, using the image of the "snake on a stick" from Numbers 21. Notice the parallels between what Jesus is telling Nicodemus and what the Israelites needed to do to be saved from the snakes. In both cases, there was no requirement for any kind of work or sacrifice. Rather, they were simply required to believe.

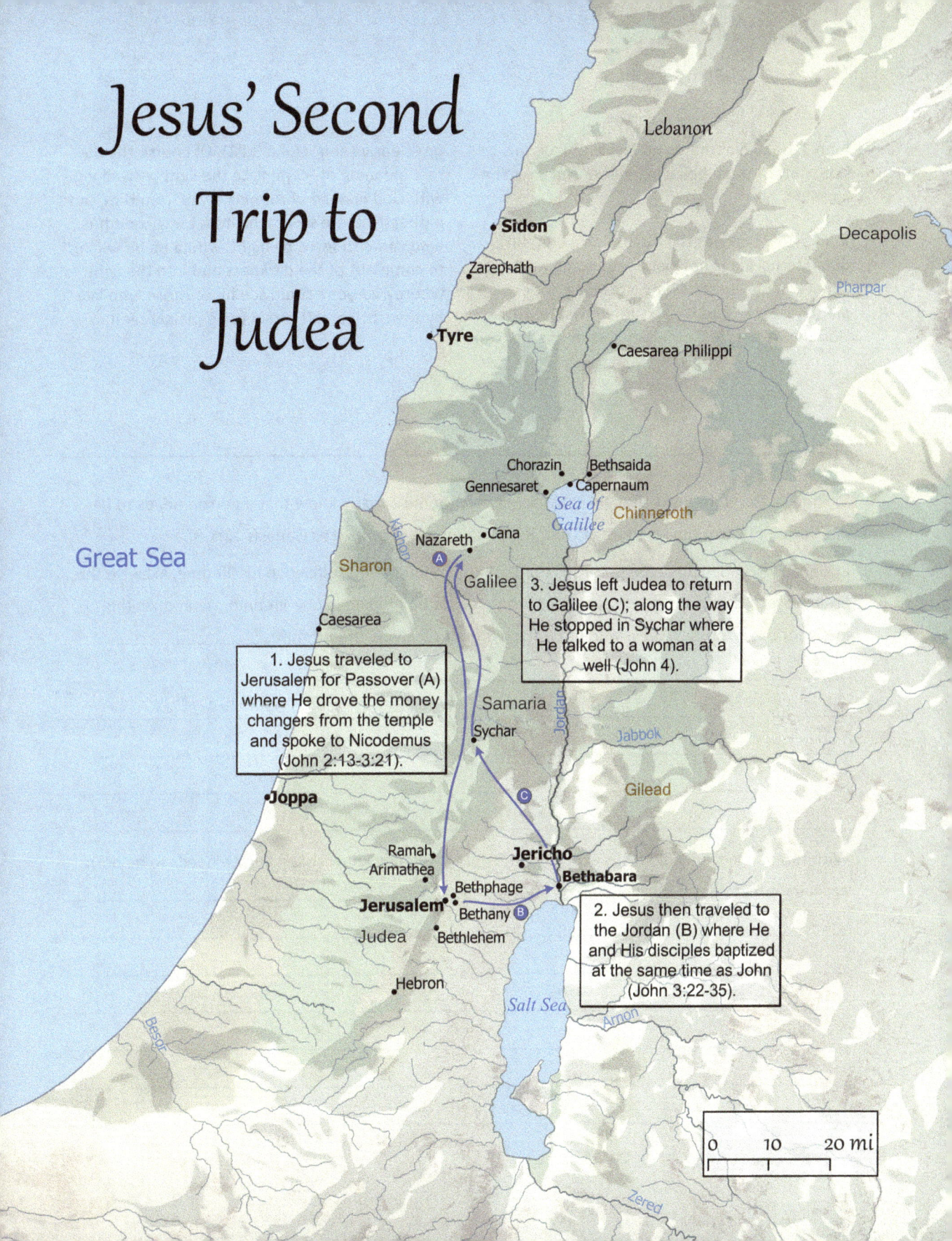

Unit 2: Jesus' Ministry Begins

John 3:16-18 elaborates on Jesus' unique mission: only through believing in Him can a person have life.

John 3:19-21 carries the discussion a step further. Eternal life is not just about going to heaven when you die; it starts right now (see, for example, John 5:24), and it's about fellowship with God that results in a different sort of life that can be "clearly seen" (John 3:21). Of course the direct meaning of "coming to the light" is walking with God instead of running away from Him, but indirectly, there's a gotcha here for Nicodemus who came to Jesus by night: would he be willing to come out of the darkness and into the light, where everyone could see him? Those who live by the truth aren't afraid to be plainly seen.

ACTIVITIES

1. Think it Through. Jesus thought that Nicodemus should already know that a person needs to be born again to enter the kingdom of God. Read Psalms 16-17 as well as Genesis 12:1-3.

In Genesis 12:1-3, God made promises to Abraham that were not fulfilled in his lifetime, likewise the Psalmist records promises in Psalms 16-17 that cannot be fulfilled in one lifetime. What does this imply for the future for those who have died without receiving the promises? _____

_____
_____
_____
_____
_____

With this in mind, why did Jesus expect Nicodemus to already know that a person needs to be born again in order to enter the kingdom of God? _____

_____
_____
_____
_____
_____
_____

2. Draw It. In the space below, draw an illustration that captures the analogy between the snake on a stick and Jesus on the cross (see John 3:14 and Numbers 21).

Unit 2: Jesus' Ministry Begins

EVALUATION

1. Why did Jesus cause such a ruckus in the temple, running out the money changers and animal sellers? _____
_____
_____

2. Why would Jesus not entrust Himself to those who believed in Him? _____
_____
_____
_____

3. What did Nicodemus think of Jesus before the conversation started? _____
_____
_____

4. Why does a person have to be born again in order to enter the kingdom of God? _____
_____
_____

5. What is the point of comparison that Jesus was driving at in John 3:14? _____
_____
_____
_____
_____

6. What was the challenge to Nicodemus in John 3:19-21? _____
_____
_____
_____
_____

Lesson 2.6

Translation of John 2:1-21

*Singular uses of "you" are in plain text. Plural uses are in bold. For example, verse 7 should be read "Do not marvel that I said to you, '**You** (plural) must be born again.'"*

¹There was a man of the Pharisees named Nicodemus, a ruler of the Jews. ² This man came to Jesus by night and said to Him, "Rabbi, we know that You are a teacher come from God; for no one can do these signs that You do unless God is with him."

³ Jesus answered and said to him, "Most assuredly, I say to you, unless one is born again, he cannot see the kingdom of God."

⁴ Nicodemus said to Him, "How can a man be born when he is old? Can he enter a second time into his mother's womb and be born?" ⁵ Jesus answered, "Most assuredly, I say to you, unless one is born of water and the Spirit, he cannot enter the kingdom of God. ⁶ "That which is born of the flesh is flesh, and that which is born of the Spirit is spirit. ⁷ "Do not marvel that I said to you, '**You** must be born again.' ⁸ "The wind blows where it wishes, and you hear the sound of it, but cannot tell where it comes from and where it goes. So is everyone who is born of the Spirit."

⁹ Nicodemus answered and said to Him, "How can these things be?"

¹⁰ Jesus answered and said to him, "Are you the teacher of Israel, and do not know these things? ¹¹ "Most assuredly, I say to you, We speak what We know and testify what We have seen, and you do not receive Our witness. ¹² "If I have told **you** earthly things and **you** do not believe, how will **you** believe if I tell **you** heavenly things? ¹³ "No one has ascended to heaven but He who came down from heaven, that is, the Son of Man who is in heaven. ¹⁴ "And as Moses lifted up the serpent in the wilderness, even so must the Son of Man be lifted up, ¹⁵ "that whoever believes in Him should not perish but have eternal life. ¹⁶ "For God so loved the world that He gave His only begotten Son, that whoever believes in Him should not perish but have everlasting life. ¹⁷ "For God did not send His Son into the world to condemn the world, but that the world through Him might be saved.

¹⁸ "He who believes in Him is not condemned; but he who does not believe is condemned already, because he has not believed in the name of the only begotten Son of God. ¹⁹ "And this is the condemnation, that the light has come into the world, and men loved darkness rather than light, because their deeds were evil. ²⁰ "For everyone practicing evil hates the light and does not come to the light, lest his deeds should be exposed. ²¹ "But he who does the truth comes to the light, that his deeds may be clearly seen, that they have been done in God."

LESSON 2.7

The Woman at the Well

UNIT 2

NOTES TO THE TEACHER

Lesson Theme - The water and food of the New Covenant: life and divine mission
Jesus would not entrust Himself to Nicodemus because he didn't really get what Jesus was up to... he didn't even understand the necessity of the new birth! This lesson is about Jesus' mission and how His disciples can take part in it.

Historical background
The story of the woman at the well took place on Jesus' journey back up to Galilee where He had begun preaching approximately a year after the start of His ministry. The usual route taken by Jews to Galilee avoided the region of Samaria. The Samaritans were not Jews by ancestry. When the Assyrians conquered the northern kingdom in 722 B.C., the people of Israel were carried off into captivity and the Assyrians brought foreigners to settle in the region. Since these foreigners were now living in Yahweh's land, God expected them to worship Him, so He sent lions into their land until a prophet taught them to worship the Lord. They continued to worship their idols alongside Yahweh for a time, but eventually gave up on the idols and worshiped Yahweh alone. But since they didn't have a shared history with Israel, they developed their own version of Yahweh worship; this included their own version of the Pentateuch and their own mountain of worship (Gerizim).

In the postexilic period, the Jews who returned to the land during the time of the Babylonians and Persians had a series of rough interactions with the Samaritans (see OT Lesson 9.4) and as

OVERVIEW

Jesus met a Samaritan woman at Jacob's well and offered her living water. After a brief conversation with Jesus, she believed He was the Messiah, drank deeply of the living water, and went to tell her whole town about the man she met at the well. The disciples had also drank of that water but failed to tell a single person in Sychar that the Messiah stood just outside their town by the well. Jesus issued a challenge to them: eat the food of God—do His will and join in the harvest.

SOURCE MATERIAL

- John 4:1-42

a result, had a strained relationship with them. Eventually, the Jews developed a hatred of the Samaritans, especially under the influence of the Pharisees whose emphasis on purity caused them to reject anyone who didn't worship the same way they did. The tension was so strong between them that the Jews would avoid Samaria altogether, taking an eastern route instead of traveling the more direct route when going from Jerusalem to Galilee.

Narrative background
To illustrate, consider the following scene: a bright sun shines overhead on a deserted dusty road in a western town. A hot breeze blows a tumbleweed across the road while the townspeople peer through windows and around corners... what happens next? Of course, its a duel

Unit 2: Jesus' Ministry Begins

OBJECTIVES

Feel...

- awe at Jesus' way of speaking to the woman at the well and His compassion for her.
- gratitude that the gospel is for everybody, even this Samaritan woman.

Understand...

- the historical background to the tension between Jews and Samaritans.
- the Old Testament background to the "woman at the well" scene.
- that this "woman at the well" scene fulfills the Old Testament pictures typologically: this woman represents the bride that Jesus came to save—the Church.
- that Jesus was trying to get the woman to understand who He was so she would take His claim to offer living water seriously.
- that we are meant to see the woman at the well as a broken down and abused woman, not an "easy" woman.
- that the woman at the well immediately began doing the will of God as soon as she received the living water.
- that the disciples failed to tell *anyone* in Sychar about Jesus.
- the difference between food and living water—invitation and challenge.

Apply this understanding by...

- evaluating your life to see if you are resting in the living water and eating the food—making sure you are in balance in regard to both the invitation to walk with Jesus and the challenge of partaking in the mission of God.

scene. Books, movies and TV shows are full of little setups like that; set-piece scenes where you know what's about to happen. In the same way, the scene we see in this passage (a man meeting a woman at a well) is a well-known biblical set-piece.

Throughout the Old Testament we have "woman at the well" scenes. Isaac found a bride (by proxy) at a well; she drew water for the servant (who was there on Isaac's behalf) and his camels. Jacob met Rachel at a well, but this time he watered *her* sheep (Gen 29). In Exodus 2, Moses met his bride, Zipporah, at a well. He not only watered her flocks, he rescued her from hostile shepherds who had run her and her flocks away from the well. In each case, the man had traveled away from his homeland and met a foreign woman. Details aside, when a man met a woman at a well, a marriage was soon to follow.

Jesus met a woman at a well
Likewise, Jesus met a woman at a well as He traveled in a foreign land. In their initial exchange, Jesus asked this woman to draw water for Him like Rebekah had for Isaac's servant. She was shocked; and truly, this was a scandalous interaction in that day: a Jew talking to a Samaritan woman? And asking her for water? This kind of interaction between a Jew and a Samaritan was unheard of. But Jesus was not really interested in getting water from her; that was just a conversation starter. He intended to offer her *living* water (John 4:10).

Notice that the question He was putting before her had to do with His identity: "If you knew the gift of God, and who it is who says to you, 'Give Me a drink'" (John 4:10). She got it; He was claiming to be someone important. Jesus was offering water, and He didn't even have a bucket to draw it out of the well with. Jacob had both dug the well at which they were standing and drawn water there; the people of Sychar had water because of Jacob. So she posed the question, "Are You greater than our father Jacob?" (John 4:12). The challenge was on the table; if the Jew she was talking to was greater than Jacob, then, "Give me this water," the woman said (John 4:15).

Jesus explained further that the water He was offering was spiritual water, welling up to eternal life such that one would never again need to drink. The woman certainly got it by then: Jesus was talking about life, not liquid. But she played along, "Sir, give me this water, that I may not thirst, nor come here to draw" (John 4:15).

At this point, Jesus appeared to change the subject by asking her to get her husband and come back (John 4:16); but remember, the challenge that was on the table was for Jesus to prove that He was greater than Jacob and therefore able to make good on His offer to give greater water than Jacob did. In this brief exchange, Jesus was able to sum up the story of her life.

At first read, it sounds like Jesus was saying she was an easy woman who would just give herself to any man who came along. There *might* be some truth in that, but it is certainly not the main point here. In that culture, a wife could not initiate divorce, *ever*. A husband, however, could initiate divorce for *any* reason (in fact, it was quite common for a man to divorce his wife for not bearing him children). Moreover, there were no jobs for women in that culture, so she would need to find a husband to support her. However, a woman who had been divorced was significantly less desirable and would probably end up married to a less than desirable husband. The woman of Sychar was caught in a cycle: she needed a husband to survive, but each husband was worse than the previous. She had been abused, discarded and abandoned.

She didn't get it yet, but Jesus was not just a prophet able to tell her about her past; He was the perfect Bridegroom there to redeem this abused bride at the well. He was greater than Jacob (who had worked 14 years for the bride he met at a well), because He was going to die for His bride so that she might have life.

At this point, the woman did start to see that Jesus was someone important, but she was not yet sure who (John 4:19-20). The dividing line between Jews and Samaritans was sharp and bright. Jesus, by simply talking to this woman, had already transgressed that barrier, but the woman wanted to see how far He was willing to go. Was this Bridegroom here to redeem Jews, Samaritans or both?

Jesus' response was neither ecumenical or sectarian. He validated the Jewish priority on Jerusalem and their claim as the source of salvation without invalidating the reality of the Samaritans' worship of Yahweh. God was the God of the Jews, but *they* didn't own *Him*. Ultimately, Jesus told her, God was not nearly as interested in where the worship took place, but the hearts of the worshipers (John 4:21-24).

His answer may sound trivial to us (mostly because we've heard it so many times), but it was a barrier-busting response in that culture. It was a response loaded with wisdom and authority. It was the kind of response the Messiah, the Bridegroom of the world, would give. She got it: "'I know that Messiah is coming' (who is called Christ). 'When He comes, He will tell us all things.' Jesus said to her, 'I who speak to you am He'" (John 4:25-26).

Jesus taught the disciples about the Father's work
Just then the disciples returned and were shocked to find Jesus talking to a Samaritan

woman, but they keep their mouths shut (John 4:27). Meanwhile, the woman, having met Jesus and having drunk the living water, dropped her water jar and headed back to town, told the townspeople about Him and led them out to meet Him (John 4:28-30).

While the people of Sychar made their way out toward them, Jesus had a few words with His disciples who had just been to town but had failed to tell anyone there that the Messiah stood just outside their city. Like Nicodemus, they didn't really get what Jesus' mission was and therefore weren't able to participate in it.

The disciples ignored the woman who had just heard from Jesus, dropped her water jar, and headed back to town, and they offered Jesus some food (John 4:31). Jesus told them that He had food that they didn't even know about (John 4:32). If living water is partaking of the life of God, eternal life, then the food of Jesus is taking part in the mission of God. The disciples had the water but not the food. The woman, to the shame of His disciples, already had both.

Shortly after Jesus and the disciples' conversation, people from Sychar began to arrive. The harvest was ready, prepared by Jesus and the woman's labors, but the disciples also got to take part in the joy of the harvest. How much more joy would it have been for them to take part in God's mission from the beginning?

Notice the difference between life and mission; water and food. The gift of water is God's calling into a person's life, requiring nothing of the believer except that he believe. Eating the food of God means doing His will. The living water that Jesus offered the woman was the *invitation* that made room for the *challenge* of taking part in the mission of God. The woman at the well hardly even needed the challenge issued to her; it naturally flowed out of her. The disciples, on the other hand, received a stiff challenge (even a rebuke) to take part in His mission.

APPLICATION

Jesus invited the woman at the well into a relationship with Him and gave His disciples a challenge to take part of the mission of God. The invitation is about rest; knowing God. The challenge is about working out of that rest. The disciples walked with Jesus; they were living in that rest daily, but didn't put it into practice and work out of it. Likewise, God calls us to work, but not until we rest in Him.

This leads to two sets of questions. First, and most importantly, are you resting in Christ? Are you at peace with God? Do you know God's forgiveness and acceptance of you? If you aren't walking with God, all your work will be an attempt to earn His acceptance rather than an outworking of your relationship with Him.

The second question is only for those who are resting in God—those who have said yes to His invitation to living water. Are you taking part in God's work? To those who are resting in Him, working for Him is a source of life—it is food. Take part in the work of God and find joy by fulfilling His purpose for your life on earth.

ACTIVITIES

1. Journal Time: Outcasts. Write a paragraph in the space below about a person (or group of people) you know who is like the Samaritan woman (an outcast whom others look down upon). Write some specific ways you can make this person feel welcome in the family of God despite their differences or past failures just like Jesus did for the Samaritan woman. This person could be an unpopular kid at school, a difficult neighbor, a family member or an entire group such as the homeless or people of a different race._____

_____
_____
_____
_____
_____
_____
_____
_____
_____

2. Journal Time: Jesus' Food. Jesus described obedience to God's will as "food" or satisfying to the soul. Write in your the space below reflecting on the following.

Think of a time when you obeyed God's will. Describe the situation and write how it was satisfying to you._____

_____
_____
_____
_____
_____

Unit 2: Jesus' Ministry Begins

Think of a time when you did not obey God's will. Describe the situation and write how it was dissatisfying. _____

_____

_____

_____

_____

_____

_____

_____

_____

_____

_____

_____

Jesus said, "The harvest truly is great, but the laborers are few" (Luke 10:2). It is always God's will for us to be workers in the harvest field. Pray for God to reveal a "harvest field" where you can work with Him, thus doing His will and being satisfied with His "food." _____

_____

_____

_____

_____

_____

_____

_____

_____

_____

_____

_____

EVALUATION

1. Why did the Jews hate the Samaritans so much? _____
_____
_____
_____
_____

2. Where in the Old Testament have we seen "woman at the well" stories? _____
_____
_____

3. What do these stories have in common? _____
_____

4. How does this scene with Jesus and the Samaritan woman fulfill those Old Testament pictures? ____
_____
_____
_____
_____

5. What does the fact that this woman had had five husbands tell us about her? _____
_____

6. What is the "living water" that Jesus was offering to the woman? _____
_____

7. When she believed in Jesus what did she immediately begin to do? _____
_____

8. How were the disciples doing on this point? _____
_____

9. What is the "food" that Jesus told His disciples about? _____
_____

www.ingramcontent.com/pod-product-compliance
Lightning Source LLC
Chambersburg PA
CBHW081337080526
44588CB00017B/2658